Machine Embroidery 101

Complete Guide to Downloading, Stabilizing, Hooping, and Stitching

Joi Mahon

Landauer Publishing

Machine Embroidery 101

Landauer Publishing, *https://landauer.foxchapelpublishing.com*, is an imprint of Fox Chapel Publishing Company, Inc.

Project Team
Editorial Director: Brian Hurley
Acquisitions Editor: Amelia Johanson
Editor: Christa Oestreich
Designer: Wendy Reynolds
Proofreader: Gretchen Bacon

Shutterstock used: AlenaBalotnik (page 90, top)

ISBN 978-1-63981-154-0

Library of Congress Control Number: 2026940779

Printed in China
First printing

MIX
Paper | Supporting responsible forestry
FSC® C217957
FSC www.fsc.org

Contents

Welcome to the Wonderful World of Sewing Machine Embroidery

If you are new to this delightful art, then get ready, because once you have embroidered your first design, you will find that one is never enough. This book is a valuable resource for your sewing studio, covering all the key elements of machine embroidery, practical tips, real workroom examples, and an entire chapter on how to approach common embroidery scenarios.

The key to success with embroidery is knowing how to plan your project and how to make the right selections. Today, the technology in our machines makes it so easy to change the settings for embroidery; the designs are extremely detailed and lifelike, and you can scan and digitize your own artwork into the machine; the hoops are larger; the threads are more advanced; and stabilizers are better and come with more options. The list goes on. Having a guide to all these options can be a lifeline for newbies and a valuable resource for experienced sewers.

When embroidery machines came out, I wanted one to elevate my sewing projects. I had

Bobier Photography

This whimsical dragon quilt was created by Morgan Mahon, my daughter. This design coordinates fabrics and threads with the book covers it was inspired by.

HOW TO USE THIS BOOK

For the purpose of this book, we are going to assume you have a sewing machine with embroidery capabilities and that your machine is serviced and in good working order. You will need to reference your machine manual for your specific embroidery feet, features, and settings. Since there are a variety of machine brands, it would be difficult to address them all here, but we will cover many of the selections in embroidery through this book, and you should easily be able to apply and adapt them to your machine and sewing.

With unlimited design options and fabric/project combinations, you will be able to use this book as a guide to plan and select the right "ingredients" for the perfect embroidery every time. Pay close attention to the topics of basic embroidery selections, thread types, needle choices, and fabric and stabilizer prep to ensure success. Utilize these guides for foolproof decisions every time.

The design gallery is sure to inspire you, and the scenarios in Chapter 7 further aid in applying all you have learned. In Chapter 2, I will show you my time-tested guidelines for planning popular sewing projects that will ensure success every time.

If you are brand-new to embroidery—maybe you purchased an embroidery machine, and it is still in the box because it is intimidating (I have been there)—no worries. I would suggest that you follow the basic monogram project on page 69 as a great beginner project. Select cotton fabric and stabilizer (page 37), and practice stitching this out multiple times until you are comfortable with your machine and how its embroidery features work. From there, you can try the monogram on different fabrics and then delve into any of the inspirational projects or scenarios featured throughout these pages. With embroidery, you can make the design whatever you want it to be.

a first-generation home embroidery sewing machine with the 4" x 4" (10.16 x 10.16cm) hoop. The designs came on an expensive embroidery disk you had to purchase at the store, there were no online downloads, and you would plug the disk into your machine or a converter box. All the accessories were expensive, and converting my machine to embroidery was quite a process of changing screws, feet, and settings. Nonetheless, I was hooked, and everyone received embroidered items that Christmas.

Amazing Designs sponsored a competition for embroidery featuring their designs, and although it was a total experiment throughout the process, I entered the professional division and won. My prize was $1,000 worth of embroidery designs on floppy disks, which was a huge help at the time because those disks were expensive. I still have them today just for posterity. This experiment got me hooked, and I have been adding embroidery to my designs ever since. I have grown with all the changes and resources as machine embroidery has developed into the wonderful art it is today.

I look at embroidery more than the "plop and drop" of the past. It is something everyone can do. Machine embroidery really is not even sewing. For those who cannot sew garments or quilts, the embroidery machine opens so many creative possibilities through embellishments to premade crafts, home décor, and other garment blanks. As embroidery practices have developed, I found that it can completely change the look of any piece.

I am sharing with you all the core skills to develop and improve your embroidery, and once you master a technique, you can take it beyond the basics to create even more amazing designs. If you are like me, you want to know all the key information needed to get you going and to avoid all the "fluff." Of course, navigating all the tools, accessories, threads, and techniques is nothing new. I hope this book will serve as a solid manual to help you use and enjoy your embroidery machine. What you will find is a rewarding and lifelong passion of creating infinite designs for your family, friends, and yourself to enjoy.

—Designer Joi

Gallery

A picture is worth a thousand words. These eye-catching embroidered projects convey the unlimited options that an embroidery machine can create with a single strategically placed design or a more complex variation that features multiple designs and hooping. This gallery is sure to inspire your next project.

Custom Floral Embroidered Pageant Gown

Embroidery Designs: Radiant Roses by Laurie Snow Hein for OESD (80144-02 Rose 2) and Super Hoop Roses by OESD (FQ561-48).

Rosanne Plante, Mrs. Agriculture America Elite and Global Beauty Award Winner, models a custom embroidered gown created by me. This custom fabric was created by layering fabric components to build the fabric base with embroidery stitches on top to create the overall look.

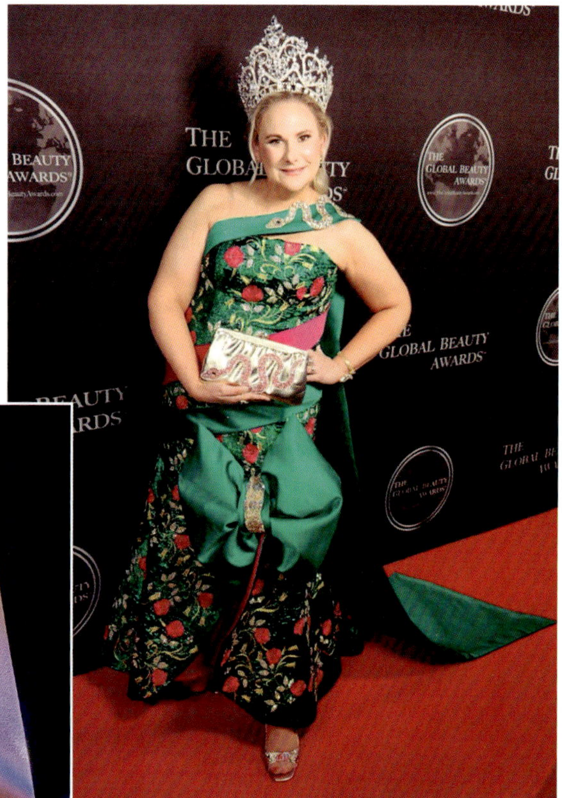

Rosanne Plante

NOTE: All embroidery design names and numbers are correct at the time of printing.

Chalkboard Alphabet

Embroidery Designs: Fashion Accents Alphabet by Joi Mahon.

Fonts are one of the most popular uses for machine embroidery with almost unlimited variations in size and style. This custom pattern, created by me, features a simplistic school look with a broken line accent and is fun for kids, monograms, and as a chalkboard fabric companion.

In-the-Hoop Stitch 'N' Turn Dolls

Embroidery Designs: Stitch 'N' Turn Dolls by OESD (12544).

Create a child's dream doll with this cute collection of doll parts. Customize the facial features, hair color, skin tone, and dress color by your choice of fabrics. Add leggings for a stylish twist. Create several friends and watch your child be entertained for hours.

Oklahoma Embroidery Supply & Design (OESD)

Embroidered Sewing Machine Bag

This all-leather sewing machine bag was created to match an embroidered leather sewing machine bodice (on page 85) that I created for a fashion show at Baby Lock Tech. This design features a variety of designs, freestanding lace, fonts, threads, and details.

Baby Layout

Embroidery Designs: Premium Hibiscus by Embroidery Legacy, fonts by OESD.

This child's collection features several popular project formats that are explored in this book: a monogram dress, a large hibiscus stitched during quilt assembly (similar to appliqué), a customized pillow blank, and allover in-the-hoop quilting.

Guys Collection: Monogrammed Vest, Necktie, and Handkerchief

Embroidery Designs: Celtic Collection by Amazing Designs.

The dapper guy's collection features a monogrammed tailored vest, necktie, handkerchief, and cuff links. The custom garment designs are by me.

Wool Celtic Coat

Embroidery Designs: Celtic Collection by Amazing Designs.

Inspired by a trip to Ireland, I created this stunning wool coat encased with Celtic knot motifs. The designs were plotted out on individual pattern pieces and strategically placed with the overall layout in mind. Most of the motifs were stitched directly onto the wool with additional motif appliqués created to place over the seam lines once the coat was sewn together.

Kenzie Banks Photography

Evy Hawkins/Sarah Jones

Embroidered Wedding Gown

Embroidery Designs: Lydia's Lace by Evy Hawkins (A Bit of Stitch).

This pattern was designed with a mama's love for a very special day! The design elements in this collection were created and used for Evy's youngest daughter's wedding, including the wedding dress! These lace designs are based on the daughter's whimsical artworks with all their lovely swoops, flourishes, and dots.

Couch Monogrammed Cushions

Embroidery Designs: Monogram M by OESD (12665-13).

Adding designs to a pillow cover is a popular use of machine embroidery for home and for gift giving. You can't always replace furniture, but you can easily swap out your décor. This quick refresh takes a little over an hour per pillow. Thanks to Miss Penelope for modeling.

Heritage Collection

Embroidery Designs: Heritage Cottage and Heritage Branch by Joi Mahon. Digitized by John Deer.

A treasured memory, this Irish cottage and tree branch were created from photos of the actual house the Mahons originated from in Ireland, along with an actual tree clipping from a small piece of land my family owns in Northern Ireland. This design is available on my website. Use this as inspiration for your own family legacy and memories to create home items that you will cherish for years to come.

Medieval Queen Design

Embroidery Designs: Feathers and Flourish by Amanda Murphy for OESD (80094).

Cosplay, costumes, and elaborate designs require a bold use of machine embroidery. This medieval queen design features brilliant flourishes created using free-standing lace techniques and wash-away stabilizers.

CHAPTER 1

The Embroidery Design

An amazing world of machine embroidery awaits you. Your journey begins with learning about the fundamental skills for successful designs. From the pictorial creative gallery offering eye-catching designs to the projects in Chapter 7, this book will help you grow and solidify your skill set for years of enjoyment and the satisfaction that creative machine embroidery provides. It all starts here!

What is Machine Embroidery?

Machine embroidery is the process where a sewing machine, which has the features and ability to do embroidery, is used to create a decorative design on fabric or a stitchable item, or is used to create independent designs, such as lace. Those designs are then affixed to the item being adorned away from the machine.

The machine may be an embroidery machine only or a combination sewing-and-embroidery machine that has a separate embroidery unit attachment. Different qualities and brands of machines have distinctive features. Just like buying a car, an important part of selecting your machine is researching what features you will need, knowing your budget, and reading reviews. A great tip when selecting any sewing machine is to define what you will be using it for and any potential features you could learn to use. If you purchase a machine that

Lace created by embroidery can be stitched directly onto an item or created as a freestanding motif for a three-dimensional effect.

Evy Hawkins

This lovely design is often used as an appliqué on children's items, making store-bought items special.

not only matches your needs and skills but also has enough extras to grow into, you will not need to replace it for at least a few years.

The purpose here is to address embroidery for the home sewer. If you run a business or want to sell your embroidery, there are commercial high-speed, multi-needle machines for use in a business setting that usually entail longer running hours on the machine and sew much faster. Maybe that will be in your future once you catch the embroidery bug.

Evy Hawkins

Strikingly beautiful monograms can be added to napkins and other home décor for a custom touch.

Unlike hand embroidery, machine embroidery is much faster and a great option for those unable to hand stitch or unable to see the needle when stitching by hand. Designs, patterns, and machine features make the possibilities endless. Like hand embroidery, machine embroidery involves stabilizing the fabric and securing it within a hoop to ensure precision during stitching. These steps will be covered in Chapters 3 and 4.

FURTHER LEARNING

For those interested in some hand stitching options, Chapter 6 in *Sewing Clothes: Elevate Your Sewing Skills* by Joi Mahon provides an array of tutorials.

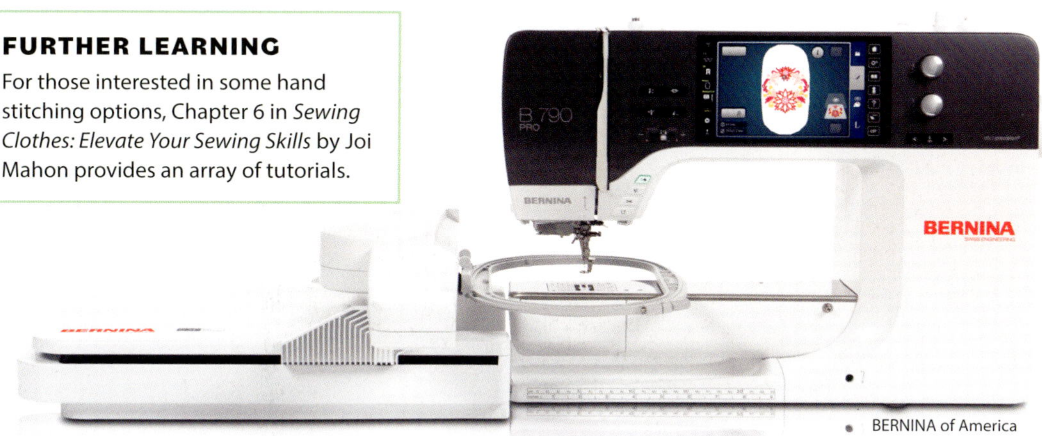

BERNINA of America

The BERNINA 790 Pro is an embroidery-only machine that features a detachable embroidery unit and multiple hoop sizes.

Embroidery Legacy

Machine embroidery designs are created with many different stitches and fills.

THE DESIGN

An embroidery design is created with beautiful threads using a combination of stitches to create texture and effect. Stitches frequently featured in machine embroidery include satin, straight, stem, blanket, feather, cross-stitch, chain, quilting, and more.

Types of embroidery designs include but are not limited to monograms, appliqués, words and quotes, motifs, lace applied or freestanding, plop and drop, allover fabric coverings, in the hoop, logos, quilting patterns, and three-dimensional. Assorted designs may suit different projects and will be discussed throughout this book. Designs can also be adjusted using your machine's editing features, such as changing size, creating mirror images, or rotating (see pages 24–26).

Where Do I Get an Embroidery Design?

Chances are your embroidery machine is preloaded with an assortment of proprietary designs that fit a variety of projects from clothing to home décor. Your machine brand may also offer tutorials that feature those specific preloaded designs, as they may have been designed specifically for that machine and its features.

As your interest and skills grow and when you see the unlimited designs available, you will want to expand your collection and options. These days, the most common way to acquire an embroidery design is a simple download from a reputable embroidery website. The design is downloaded onto your computer as a digital file. It is now easy and affordable to buy embroidery designs online, with single patterns typically available for just a few dollars. Simply make sure the designs you purchase are compatible with your machine format (see page 15) and hoop size.

It is worth noting that there are still companies that offer designs and design packs on a tangible device that you can order through the mail. Things like disks, CD-ROMs, and flash drives hold designs on them that transfer to the computer or embroidery machine. With older floppy disks that are preloaded with designs, you can purchase an inexpensive floppy drive or CD drive that plugs into your computer. Insert the device into the drive and treat it like you are downloading from a website (see page 17).

WHAT I CAN AND CANNOT DO WITH A DESIGN

Integrity in sewing should be your utmost priority. Designers make a tiny profit from individual designs, so do not cheat them on their livelihood. While not legal advice, here are some general rules for embroidery design use:

- **Buying designs:** Do not borrow designs others have purchased for their own sewing projects. Purchase your own copy and pay for any designs you are using. Most designs in home sewing are meant for individual, personal use.
- **Selling pieces:** While you can certainly stitch designs on gifts for others and make multiples, if you plan to create a line of products where you stitch multiples of the same design with the intent to sell for profit as a business, you should contact the designer for a license.
- **Selling designs:** You cannot resell a purchased design as your own and especially do not take credit for others' work.
- **Modifying:** Embroidery designers usually do not allow designs to be modified beyond the accepted machine basics, such as the examples on page 24.
- **Verifying:** Most importantly, purchase from a reputable brand for quality and no copyright infringement.

WHAT DO I EMBROIDER?

Almost anything can be embellished with embroidery, either sewn on directly or created independently from the item and affixed. Everything from bags, towels, quilts, clothing, shoes, and toys to fabrics, ornaments, and premade blanks are enhanced with designs featuring fun, whimsical, contemporary, and monochromatic themes. There is an embroidery aesthetic for everyone.

You will see a variety of projects throughout this book that represent the unlimited possibilities of machine embroidery: a monogram T-shirt, butterfly on denim jacket, bunny on fleece blanket, etc.

Note copyright! We all love our favorite movie character, sports team, and recognizable brand logo. Unfortunately, it is all too common to see crafty folk copying these legally copyrighted items and selling on popular craft platforms. It is not always intentional. Sometimes creators do not understand the idiosyncrasies of proprietary items.

As an example, I will use my business. While I may be a small fish compared to a big corporation, I do own and have paid for the legal copyright on my brand Designer Joi, the artwork that goes with it, along with some other products I am affiliated with. I never give anyone permission to recreate my logos on any product at any time. I would not expect to go to a website and see my artwork being sold by someone else as an embroidery design or printed on a T-shirt, but this happens with our favorite products all the time.

While it may be difficult to enforce, be careful supporting designers who copy legally protected property on popular creative online platforms. Copying and not paying for resources that you use, even if digital, affects the longevity of creative businesses and overall adds to price increases for everyone. Reputable sources are key to avoiding this. If you have any questions or need permission, simply consult the source for usage guidelines specific to their designs and intellectual property. Often, they are delighted to work with you and support your creative endeavors. Plus, it is just more fun and meaningful when you have your own original ideas.

MACHINE FILE FORMATS: A DIGITAL LANGUAGE

When purchasing a design for your machine to stitch, you will need to select the file format that matches your machine format. The format is like the digital language of your embroidery machine. This file holds the information your embroidery machine needs to create the design, such as what type of stitch to use, design size, how many colors are used, and where the stitches go. The design needs to match the format for the machine to read and stitch it successfully.

Each file format relates to unique software put out by the embroidery machine company, which comes with your purchase. When you open the design, it will default to that program.

Like the differences in Macs and PCs, embroidery machines require translated files to read them. To find out what format your machine is, you will need the machine brand and the model number. Some machine brands can read or use multiple file formats. Most embroidery designs that you purchase will be available in most of the popular formats or offer the option to select the right version for you. There are also software programs that can convert from one version to another. Reference your machine manual to see what formats work best on your model. Note that some older models use different formats than the newer machines. Additionally, there are other formats that are not listed here.

If you are having difficulties getting a design to work with your machine, make sure you have the correct format and that the size of the design also works with your machine hoop size (see page 46). The more times a design is converted, the more possibilities that modifications and distortions are made to the design.

LIST OF FORMATS

Different formats are proprietary to individual brands and have distinctive features and capabilities, although some will work on various machines. Simply check to see what your machine prefers. The most common file formats for embroidery designs and corresponding machines are:

- ART (BERNINA)
- DST (multi-needle and commercial machines)
- EMB (Wilcom)
- EXP (BERNINA)
- HUS (HUSQVARNA® VIKING®)
- JAN (Janome)
- JEF (Janome)
- PCS (PFAFF®)
- PES (Brother and Baby Lock)
- PSW (SINGER®)
- SHV (HUSQVARNA® VIKING®)
- VIP (HUSQVARNA® VIKING® and PFAFF®)
- VP3 (HUSQVARNA® VIKING®)
- XXX (SINGER®)

How to Use an Embroidery Design

DOWNLOADING AND SAVING THE DESIGN

After navigating an embroidery website and deciding what design you want, check that you have selected the correct size and format. Place it in the shopping cart and process your payment method. The important part is what happens next. While all computers and websites vary, these are standard methods for working with digital files; saving them on your computer, tablet, or phone; and knowing where the files are located. After completing the transaction, the design will be sent in one of the following ways:

- **Automatic direct download:** If this is the way your computer is set up, the design will automatically download and save as a file on your computer. You need to know where your computer is set to automatically put downloaded files, so you know where they go. Most systems have a location called "Downloads." There may also be a quick pop-up menu on the upper-right side of your internet browser or monitor that shows the download starting. (If you do not see this, you can activate a setting on your computer so it shows the files being downloaded.) Clicking on a file in this pop-up menu will usually route you to the place where the file is saved.

TIP: If you did not know that there is a specific place where files are downloaded, you may find a trove of forgotten files hanging out waiting there for you. Please check this location before you reach out to customer service with a complaint that you did not receive your design.

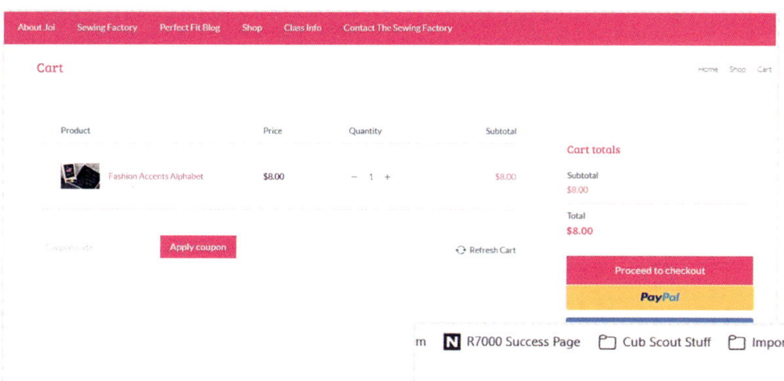

(Left) A shopping cart checkout page looks the same when buying a digital design. (Below) However, upon completion, some pages will automatically download the file. This internet browser window shows what has been downloaded.

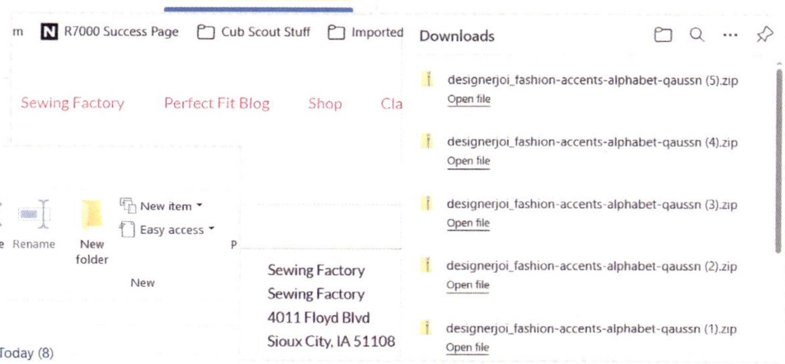

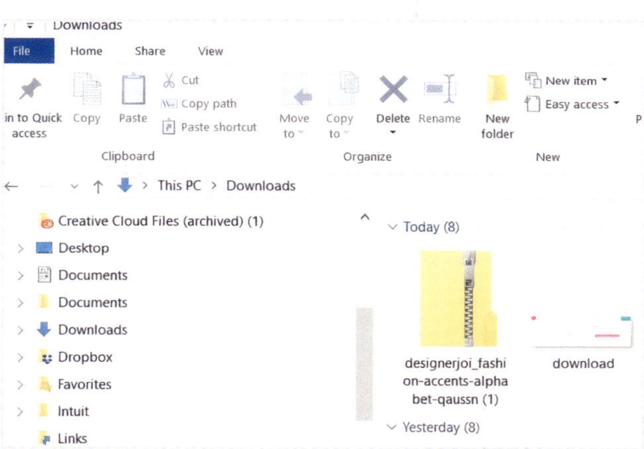

(Left) On your computer, the Downloads folder is where the files actually live.

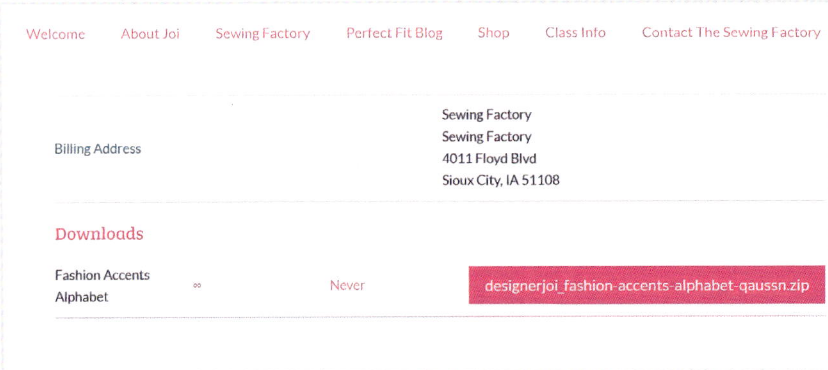

Some websites will not automatically download the design. Instead, you will need to click a button to start the download.

- **Manual direct download:** Upon completing the purchase, there may be an additional checkout page, button, or link that you manually click to start the process of saving the file to your computer. From there, the computer may follow the automatic saving steps to your Downloads folder, or it may give you the option to select where you save the file. This is ideal because you can choose the specific place it is downloaded to on your computer, and it is much harder to lose it.
- **Email with a download link:** After purchase, some websites will send you an email with a clickable link to access the design. When you click the link, the download will follow either the automatic or manual direct download steps as described above and on page 17.
- **Account access on the website:** Websites that offer customer accounts on the site usually have an Order History or Download tab where you can find your purchased designs. Log into the website, find your account information, and click to download the design to your computer. It will follow either the automatic or manual direct download steps as described above and on page 17.

ORGANIZING YOUR EMBROIDERY DESIGN FILES

Embroidery design files start to add up quickly, and many files include a variety of designs and iterations. A single pack could have over 50 elements, especially if you are using an alphabet. To avoid searching all over your device for a specific design, it is smart to create a folder where all your embroidery content is stored. To do this:

1. Create a folder on your computer, tablet, or phone called "My Embroidery." If you are still trying to visualize how this all works, think of this as a file cabinet. All this folder is doing is storing your design files. When downloading a file, select the My Embroidery folder as the location to save your designs to; or once a design is saved into your Downloads folder, move it over to the My Embroidery folder. It is beneficial to do this early in your embroidery career; a couple random designs can quickly turn into thousands of designs floating around. Move all your designs to this folder for easy navigating and searching.
2. For even better navigation, add subfolders of common design themes, such as animals, holidays, lace, appliqués, fonts, hearts, stars, etc. For example, if looking for rose embroidery, you know that sorting through the Fonts folder will not help. These destinations in the digital file cabinet are invaluable when looking for a favorite design—and a folder named "Favorites" is also a great idea!
3. Once you download a design, rename it to something recognizable. For example, instead of AD1234, change to something like "LargeRoseAppliqueAD1234." You may or may not be able to view your design in the folder, so labeling what a design file looks like will save you hours of time and frustration. It also makes it easy to search by those terms.

SAVING TO AN EXTERNAL STORAGE DEVICE

Instead of saving and storing designs on your computer, tablet, or phone hard drive, designs may be downloaded and stored on an external storage device, such as a small portable hard drive or USB flash drive. This frees up space on your computer or phone with limited storage, giving you designs on a small handheld device you can take on the go.

If you have the option to choose where the file is downloaded (manual direct download), instead of the Downloads or My Embroidery folder, select the external drive from the menu when downloading, and the designs will be saved on the device.

If your embroidery designs are on your computer and you want to move them to the external device, follow these steps:

1. Open the Downloads or My Embroidery folder on your computer.
2. Make sure your external device is inserted into the computer (usually through a USB). The icon will appear on your desktop and/or the left menu of the Finder window.
3. Select the design file in your folder and right click.
4. If you want to completely remove the design from the computer drive, select cut from the pop-up menu. If you want to keep it on the computer, select copy.
5. Select the external drive icon and right click.
6. Select paste from the pop-up menu. The design is now in your external drive. If you selected cut, then the design is also removed from your hard drive.

TRANSFERRING THE DESIGN TO THE SEWING MACHINE

Now that the purchased design is downloaded to your computer, the next step is to move the design from the computer into the embroidery machine. There are several options for how to achieve that:

- **USB cable:** Machines with cables are tethered to the computer for data transfer. A design is selected in the files, copied, and transferred to the machine using steps 1–6 at left. In step 5, select the cable name or the sewing machine name. The design is transferred to the machine, can be opened, and is ready to be stitched.
- **Flash drives and portable hard drives:** A flash drive or storage device containing designs is plugged directly into the embroidery machine to transfer a design. You might need a USB adapter, depending on what outlet your machine

Oklahoma Embroidery Supply & Design (OESD)

Insert the USB flash drive (as shown) or external drive cord into the embroidery machine.

Like a laptop, your embroidery machine will have a USB port somewhere on the side. This is where you plug in the portable drive to load your designs.

has. I also like using an adapter for extra length, so I can insert into a USB end right in front of me rather than searching or straining to find the outlet.

- **Wi-Fi:** If your devices have Wi-Fi capabilities, then you have more options of downloading and moving files. Many embroidery machines can download patterns directly onto their hard drive. No cables required. Additionally, sewing machines with Wi-Fi features can receive a design from a phone or computer, making the process even more streamlined. For this to work, the device and embroidery machine need to be on the same network.

Reference your machine manual for any specific instructions that are unique to its features and capabilities.

Digitizing Your Own Designs

WHAT IS DIGITIZING?

Digitizing is the process of taking a design idea, either a hand-drawn sketch, photograph, or computer-generated file, and converting it to a format that embroidery software can read. Knowing how a design is made helps you choose the right option for your product and identify quality tools for better sewing. While this book will not cover this topic in detail, it is important to note that digitizing is one of the tools available for further personal development of embroidery techniques.

If you are new to machine embroidery, you will rely on stock designs and basic editing directly from your embroidery machine. However, at some point, you may want to turn your ideas into custom embroidery designs for personal or business use, and there are multiple options, each yielding different results:

- **Hire a specialist:** The fastest and easiest option is to hire a skilled digitizer to create the design for you. Based on the complexity of the design, the cost will be significantly higher than a stock download. Remember, you will be hiring someone to create a custom product, so expect to pay accordingly for that service and skill.
- **Do it yourself:** Early embroidery machines required a hands-on approach to digitizing. The photo below demonstrates how to create stitches directly on fabric with an older machine—a process that highlights how far technology has come. While modern software has streamlined digitizing, the principles remain the same.

Digitizing software offers the ultimate in creative design. With all the developments in technology, digitizing is becoming more approachable to the average embroidery sewist. The software ranges from beginner versions with basic features to professional programs producing superior results, and many come with automatic functions that include options to customize each stitch design.

However, many programs lack user-friendliness or sufficient quality for creating advanced designs.

Here, Sam is digitizing right on the screen of the embroidery machine, showing it can be fun for all ages and easy to develop new skills.

Embroidery Legacy

Modern digitizing often begins on tablet or computer. Here you see stitches being plotted directly onto artwork, creating the roadmap that embroidery machines will later follow.

Understanding your software requirements and what your software requires of you—what it can and cannot do—will help you in your selection.

Who is better to address the topic of embroidery than the most award-winning embroidery digitizing expert in the world than John Deer, founder of Embroidery Legacy? John Deer has a generational legacy in developing the foundation of modern machine embroidery as we know it today. Long before computers even entered the digitizing world, John began his career apprenticing under Swiss Schiffli Master Digitizers and is the last remaining Schiffli Master still alive and teaching in North America.

John Deer says, "Embroidery may look different today with all our modern tools, but the heart of the craft has not changed. Every stitch still follows the same principles I learned decades ago from my Schiffli mentors. Technology is evolving, but the art and foundation of embroidery remain timeless."

Designs start on a screen, but they come to life on fabric! Always keep the final project in mind while you consider your design options.

STEP-BY-STEP BREAKDOWN

A quality embroidery design does not just happen—it is built step by step. Each stage plays a key role in how the design runs, looks, and holds up over time. Here is a simple breakdown of the process, from the first stitch plan to the polished finish, courtesy of John Deer and Embroidery Legacy.

Embroidery Legacy

1. Pathing (the roadmap). Every design begins with pathing—the "blueprint" for how the stitches will run. Good pathing minimizes trims and jump stitches while also spreading out the stress on the fabric, so the design holds its shape. Without proper pathing, even the best stitches can cause puckering or registration issues.

Embroidery Legacy

2. Underlay (the foundation). Underlay stitches are the hidden framework of embroidery. They stabilize the fabric, reduce puckering, and give top stitches something to grip. A solid underlay ensures fills and satins sit smoothly and look professional.

EMBROIDERY EDUCATION

Curious about digitizing but not sure where to start? A class is probably the best way to learn, as it can be a lot to figure out on your own. In-person and online classes are available, such as through Embroidery Legacy (www.embroiderylegacy.com). They have a library of courses and workshops to try, including a free Digitizing 101 course.

Embroidery Legacy

3. Fill stitches (the shape). Fill stitches add coverage and create the body of the design. Planning stitch angles and density properly helps avoid distortion from push and pull. When done right, fills give the embroidery a strong, balanced look.

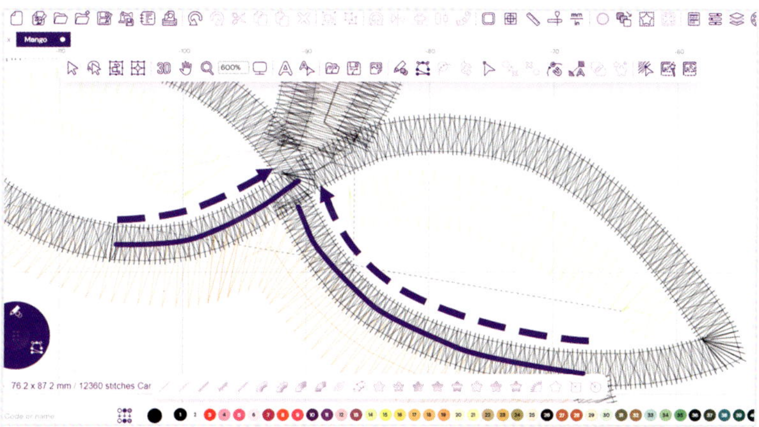

Embroidery Legacy

4. Run stitches (the detail). Run stitches bring minute details and delicate lines to life. They are perfect for shading, texture, or outlining small elements that fill and satin cannot capture. Runs also act as invisible travel stitches, keeping the design efficient and clean.

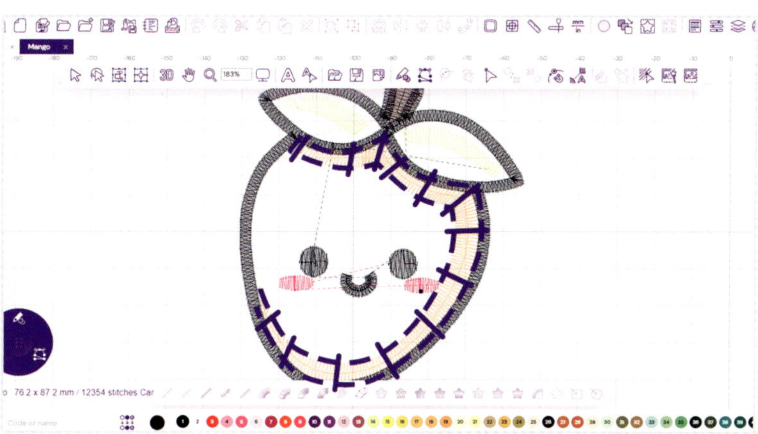

Embroidery Legacy

5. Satin stitches (the finish). Satin stitches are the bold, polished finish of a design. They are often used for borders, letters, or crisp details that make embroidery pop. A good satin stitch adds definition and ties the whole design together.

Basic Design Editing on Your Machine

All embroidery machines include basic design editing features commonly used in modifying designs. These functions are available directly on the machine during the process when you are setting up the design for stitching. Check your machine manual for details, but typically you will follow several steps on the Pattern Editing Screen before pressing the start button to stitch, during which your machine may prompt you with some of the following options:

Your machine offers many buttons and settings. Utilize the built-in help buttons and your machine manual to understand all its capabilities.

1. **Preview image.** Shows the design to be stitched and all the details, such as size, thread count, stitch-out time, and position keys to move the design around the hooped stitching surface.

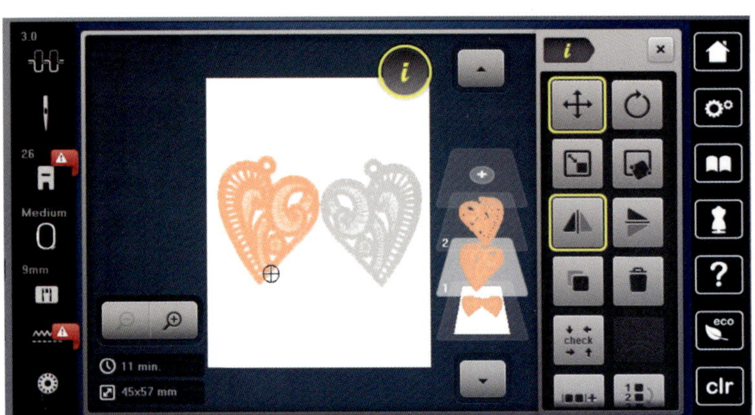

2. **Mirror image.** Flip the design to make an exact copy either vertically (up and down) or horizontally (left and right).

3. Color change. Displays how many thread colors are in the design. You can change colors on screen to test other combinations prior to stitching.

4. Monochromatic. Sets the design to stitch all in one color instead of using color changes.

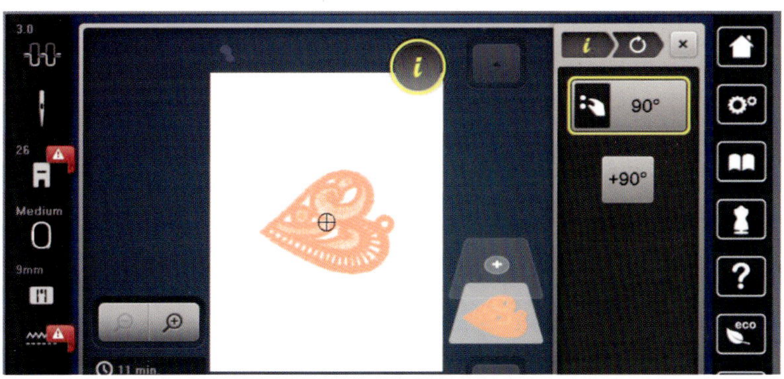

5. Rotate. Change the position of the design by 45, 90, or 180 degrees. Adding fine adjustments to the angle, you can also position the design by 1 to 359 degrees on the hooped project.

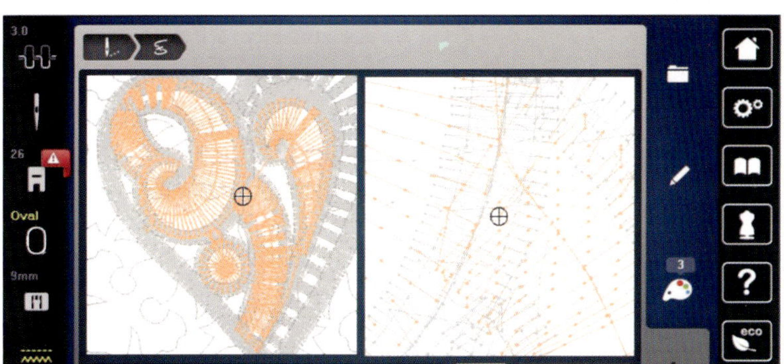

6. Stitch advance. This setting is used for moving forward or backward on the embroidery stitching to bypass parts of a design. Or you can go back to restitch missed stitches after a thread break.

7. Layering. Combining multiple patterns in a single hooped layout, such as adding a name over a larger monogram. Additional options of alignment include straight, curved, and angled placement.

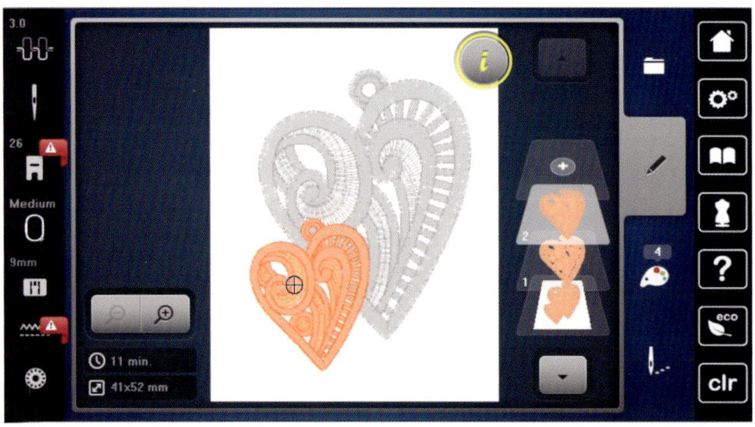

8. Scale and sizing. Increase or decrease a design vertically, horizontally, or proportionally. Adjusting the spacing of characters is included, but these adjustments are limited in scope.

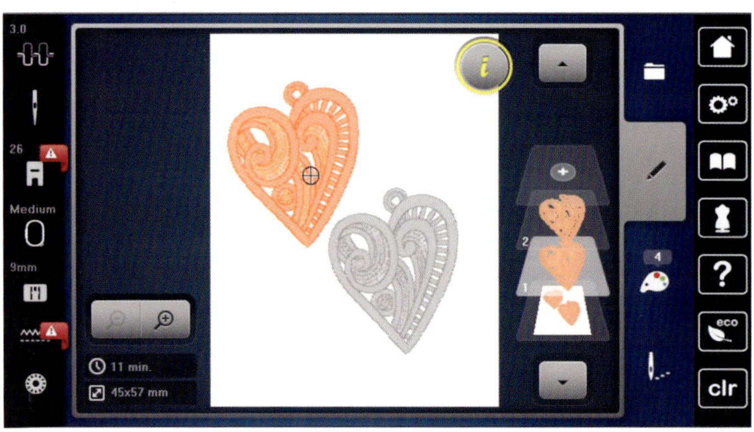

9. Duplicating. Make an exact copy of a design. This technique is used in creating a continuous border or multiple designs.

Embroidery Supplies and Scissors

The joy of embroidery is that once you have a machine and its basic parts, it is quite an affordable form of sewing. While there are always gadgets and tools marketed to the embroidery enthusiast, you will not need a lot of extra sewing supplies beyond what you already have in your sewing stash. To start, all you need are the items you are stitching on, thread, stabilizer, and basic sewing supplies like a ruler and scissors. After that, you can add in all the extra gadgets as you grow your skills and interests. Later in this book, we will take an in-depth look at needles, threads, and stabilizers, but first let us focus on an overview of essential tools you will use in all projects.

- **Embroidery needles and threads:** The embroidery machine needle has an eye that is enlarged, so there is less stress on the thread passing through the eye. This will help prevent fraying due to the high friction of the rapid movement and speed at which it stitches the fabric. Embroidery needles are available in chrome and titanium. Needles are covered more in Chapter 6.
- **Embroidery hoops:** Your machine will come with the basic hoops that work with your brand. These hoops are necessary to support the fabric during stitching, hold the fabric taut, and prevent puckering and slipping. Hoops will have guidelines that aid in placement of the design on the fabric. They come in a variety of shapes and sizes, and some have magnetic features. Learn more about hooping in Chapter 5.
- **Hooping stations:** These innovative gadgets aid in positioning items being embroidered for rapid hooping and help when creating multiples of the same item, especially in a business setting. For example, you would probably want a hooping station for shirts.
- **Hoop tape and grippers:** Tape for embroidery is used around the edge of the hoop to help prevent slippage of the fabric during stitching. The tape is placed on the edge of the hoop

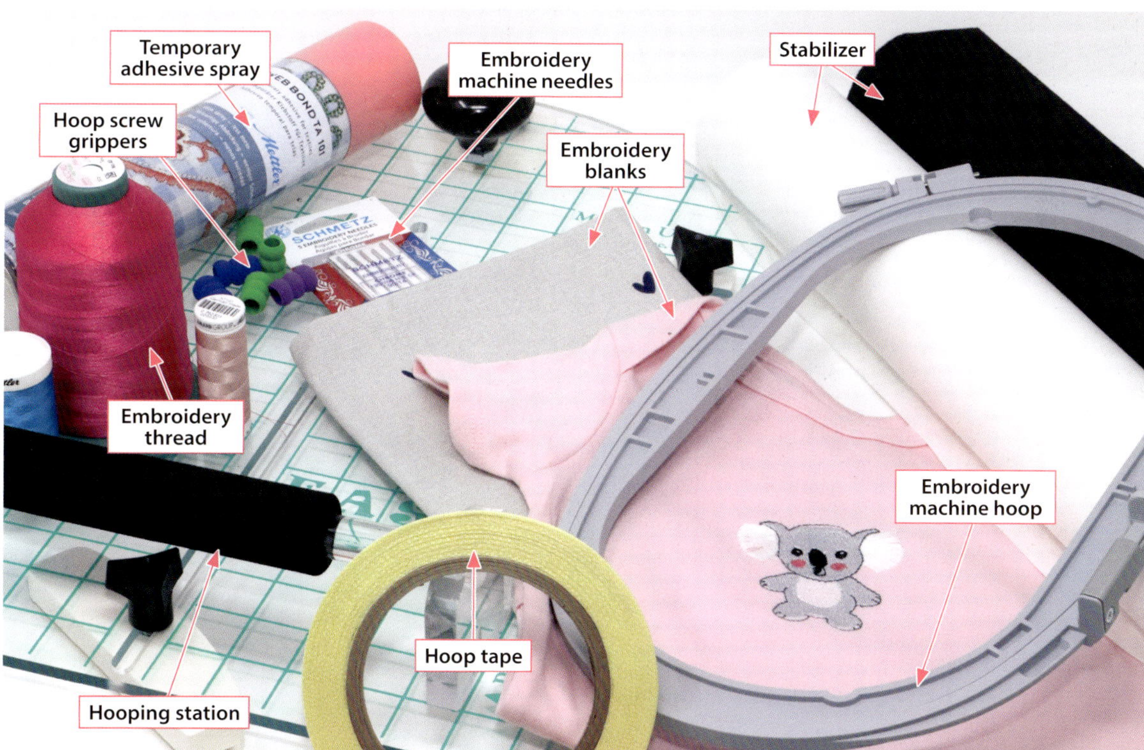

touching the fabric, which is usually the top hoop. It is sticky enough to be used multiple times. With tapes designed specifically for embroidery hoops, we no longer rely on basic double-sided tape of the past.

- **Embroidery stabilizer:** Stabilizer is the layer placed underneath an item to support the stitches. New innovations in stabilizers provide just the right option for any embroidery scenario. There are sew-in, tearaway, fusible, mesh, heavyweight, lightweight, and wash-away to name a few. More information about stabilizers is found in Chapter 3.
- **Embroidery blanks:** Machine embroidery can be placed on almost any object from towels and shirts to bags and fabrics. With the growth of the embroidery industry, there has been growth in items specifically designed for embroidery. These items, called blanks, also come in all shapes, colors, and sizes. There are companies that specialize in blanks, which can include anything from bags, shirts, key rings, collars, and jewelry to stuffed animals, towels, lunch bags, and more.
- **Temporary spray adhesive:** Slippery fabrics or fabrics with loft, such as terry cloth, may require a little extra help to stay in place during embroidery. Temporary spray adhesives are used to hold the stabilizer and fabrics together for a brief time during embroidery. The stabilizer then is steamed away, washed away, or fades away over a brief period. This is an invaluable tool in embroidery. It can leave a residue, so avoid fabrics that may spot, like silks, and make sure you select the spray adhesive specific for embroidery.

EMBROIDERY SCISSORS

It is important to note how specific shears designed for embroidery can assist in better results throughout the process. There are many shears available for the various sewing tasks that we encounter. Since embroidery features a high density and large quantity of stitches, it is imperative to have a quality pair of fine-point scissors. It is also important to have scissors that curve away from the stitching to prevent accidentally clipping the thread jumps.

Devin Head, representative from Kai Scissors, says that the curved blade used in embroidery allows the scissors to sit directly on top of your project without the risk of poking any holes or getting snagged. An example of this is the 4-Inch Double Curved Scissors (N5100C). Devin also recommends a sharp point. Some blunt scissors are for safety, but when you need to get into a small area or under a tight jump stitch, the points are invaluable.

The N5130DC are blunt scissors, but Devin likes to highlight the shape of this product. The curved handle helps raise the scissors over the edge of an embroidery frame, and if you have larger fingers, the holes are bigger than the N5100C.

One size truly does not fit all when it comes to sewing shears. Make sure to have fine-point shears, curved shears, and some longer blades to match the fabrics and stabilizers you will be cutting for your embroidery projects.

Kai Scissors

The side view of the N5100C scissors clearly illustrates the curved tip, which is good for cutting close to the fabric.

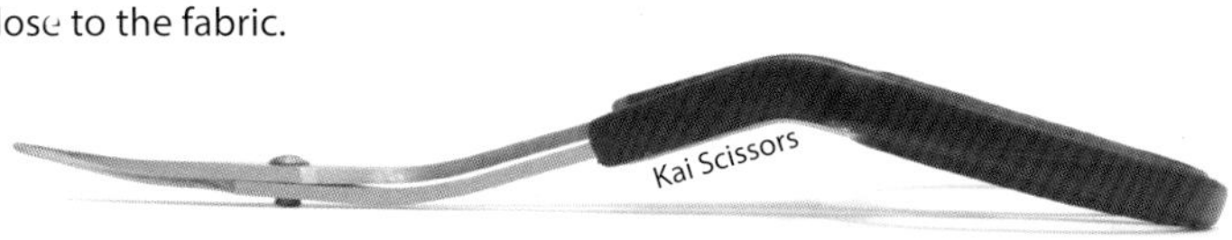

Kai Scissors

The side view of the N5130DC scissors shows the curved handle, which comfortably sits above the embroidery hoop.

CHAPTER 2

Planning Your Embroidery Project

As you explore the infinite designs available, chances are you stumbled upon something you love and are well on your way to designing a project around the embroidery. Have you ever added embroidery to a design or observed embroidery that does not lie well on a garment? Maybe the design sinks into the fabric, or the design pulls on the fibers? As a garment designer, I know the importance of planning out the fabrications that go into my designs, especially those that elevate a sewn garment to a professional-looking product. It is not enough to pick a garment or fabric, grab an embroidery stabilizer, and then start adding embroidery. With careful planning and decision-making, your embroidery will be successful every time.

Creating a Design Sample

While embroidery is almost foolproof when done correctly, it can be immensely frustrating when a design is not stitching well, the tension is off, or another issue appears. For the most common issues, review the troubleshooting section on page 102. For these solutions, we are going to assume that your machine is in good working order. If the machine is working well, any issue that will arise when stitching is due to the incorrect combination of design, fabric, stabilizer, or needle (page 64) and can be corrected with subtle adjustments to them.

TIP: The number one way to troubleshoot any embroidery issues is to test the combinations of "ingredients" before stitching your final project.

This stitch sample for the Wool Celtic Coat (page 9) was to test the compatibility of the embroidery design with the wool fabric and to see how the thread colors would stand out against the fabric.

There is no standard interfacing or stabilizer that works in every embroidery scenario. A lightweight cotton fabric (right), a stretchy knit top (center), and a dense denim jacket (left) all require different stabilizers to support the embroidery design.

SAMPLE CARD

Use the Embroidery Sample Card on the opposite page as a guide for keeping track of all your fabric and embroidery combinations. Make copies of this card, place them in a binder, and build your own library of "recipes" used in embroidery that is unique to you. Place this binder alongside this book in your workspace for easy access to settings that work with your fabric and machine. It will be an invaluable tool.

Address Your Fabric First

Most fabrics can be embroidered. Basic fabric knowledge tells us that we should take into consideration that some fabrics or materials are of better quality. Creating a sample card and utilizing the following techniques for pretreating your fabric will help either identify poor fabric choices or counter any issue, so the fabric will embroider with desired results. Remember that your embroidery will only look as good as the fabric it is on. Not all fabrics need special consideration, but for those that do, it is an easy fix.

STABILIZE THE FABRIC

Stabilizer is for supporting the embroidery stitches and may be removed after stitching. A complete guide to stabilizers is featured in Chapter 3. Adding a layer of stabilizer to support the stitching does not mean it corrects any issue with the fabric. This is not commonly addressed in embroidery education but is a major contributor to professional results.

Creating a test sample will prevent results like this showing up in your final project. This fabric needed some stability prior to embroidery to prevent wrinkles.

Machine Embroidery Sample Card

EMBROIDERY DESIGN NAME & NUMBER:

DESCRIPTION:

DESIGN SIZE: HOOP SIZE:

FABRIC AND PROJECT:

THREAD SELECTIONS:

NEEDLE SELECTION:

STABILIZER:

OTHER:

Attach a sample stitch out to this card for reference.

Make a new card for each variation on fabric, size, and design.

Machine Embroidery Sample Card

EMBROIDERY DESIGN NAME & NUMBER:

DESCRIPTION:

DESIGN SIZE: HOOP SIZE:

FABRIC AND PROJECT:

THREAD SELECTIONS:

NEEDLE SELECTION:

STABILIZER:

OTHER:

Attach a sample stitch out to this card for reference.

Make a new card for each variation on fabric, size, and design.

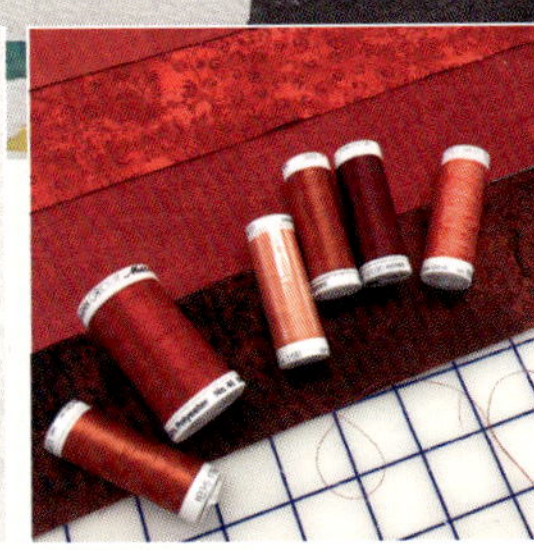

Bobier Photography

BIOGRAPHY OF STABILIZING A QUILT

Morgan was creating a quilt with a densely stitched dragon design. She purchased high-end quilting cotton from a local fabric boutique, but even though it was a top-of-the-line brand of quilt fabrics, this cotton had quite a bit of stretch to it. When she placed a variety of medium-weight stabilizers on the hoop, added the fabric, and proceeded to embroider, the design would never lie flat; it would pull around the edges.

This was not a machine tension issue. The fabric had too much give and would distort in the hoop. She applied some fusible knit interfacing to the fabric square. It did not add weight to the fabric but did stabilize the weave. Finally, the embroidery stitched beautifully.

It took her stitching the hour-long design seven times and testing the interfacings, stabilizers, and dense motif before she had the right "recipe" for her award-winning quilt project. This quilt had several hundreds of dollars of fabric and over 100 hours of work. The time and attention to detail in the selection of all components that went into this design resulted in an outstanding quilt that looked flawless.

FABRIC INTERFACINGS

Learning to address the fabric structure with fabric interfacings is different than adding embroidery stabilizer. Interfacing is used to address the fabric characteristics and stays in the project. Interfacing will stabilize the grain or stretch of a fabric, adding density to further aid in successful embroidery. But the key is that you are selecting it to assist the fabric regardless of the embroidery design.

There is a lovely assortment of interfacings for garment construction used in commonly interfaced areas like collars, pockets, and plackets. This interfacing supports the sewn areas of the garment pattern, but that is not the kind of application we are addressing here. For embroidery, we are talking about using garment interfacings to stabilize the fabric area being embroidered to support the stitches. This interfacing may cover the entire pattern piece, a part of it may be left on the fabric, or some may be removed. So, we will treat them separately.

After applying the embroidery, you will reference your pattern sewing instructions for the interfacing pieces needed to support pattern pieces. It is possible they can be the same, but that is not always the case. For example, if you are embroidering a medium-weight collar, you would need interfacing to stabilize the fabric for receiving the embroidery stitches. After adding embroidery, you may still need to add another layer of interfacing to support the actual shape of the collar roll. Sometimes adding interfacing and then embroidery stabilizer to an area being embroidered is enough. The key is testing your combinations, making a record of the results, and using your sample card for similar scenarios in the future. This takes the guesswork out of knowing if your embroidery will meet your expectations.

FABRIC EVALUATION

Setting aside the embroidery design, let us look at evaluating any fabric yardage, cut pattern pieces, or garment blanks. (For our purpose here, we will just reference "fabric" to mean anything we are embroidering). Questions you might ask about fabric include: Does it have an open weave with gaps between the yarns or are the yarns dense and tightly woven together? Does the fabric stretch because it is a knit or stretch because of the weave? Is the fabric lightweight like silk or heavy like denim?

These interfacings illustrate a variety of options available to the embroidery to help achieve the best results.

As you evaluate your fabric, add the embroidery design to the equation. Depending on your answer, you will need to add a compatible interfacing that provides a reliable fabric surface for holding the embroidery design.

NOTE: Some projects, such as lace, may even be embroidered altogether without a fabric (see page 74).

Dense designs stitch out better on stable fabric that will not distort with the considerable number of stitches and friction.

Lightweight Fabrics

Let us look at some quick combinations of fabric, interfacing, and stabilizers for lightweight and heavyweight designs. Beginning with light- to mid-weight projects, these fabrics usually require some sort of fabric interfacing prior to embroidery.

- **Cotton fabrics with stretch:** The selvage or warp grain is the most stable on basic cotton fabrics, but the weft or cross grain may have some give or outright stretch to it from the fiber used or mechanical stretch from the weave. Use a fusible weft interfacing to anchor the stretch and stabilize for stitching.
- **Sheer fabric:** It is possible to interface a sheer or opaque fabric. The goal is to stabilize but not change the look of the fabric. The best interfacing for a sheer fabric is simply using the same fabric; this provides exact match and blending. Other options include a tan ultra-light interfacing, mesh, or organza for clothing; and ultra-lightweight interfacings or fabrics for non-garments. These simple solutions provide excellent results.

Designs that are more open and less dense stitch out better on more delicate or open-weave fabrics. This design has a decorative and intentional off-center outline stitch.

Fusi-knit is an interfacing used in garment construction to stabilize the fibers of a fabric or item that may have unstable areas. It can be used on knits and wovens.

Fusible-weft is an interfacing used in garment construction that adds some reinforcement to prevent stretching in a specific direction.

Sew-in garment interfacing is used to add density and stability to a fabric in garment construction.

- **Designs cut on the bias:** Bias is when a pattern is intentionally designed on a 45-degree angle from the straight of the grain. This is usually with a lightweight fabric that creates a lovely drapey effect. Garments, such as a camisole, cowl top, or flowy skirt, feature bias. You do not want to remove the bias drape with stiff or on-grain interfacing. Using fusible knit interfacing or a lightweight interfacing cut on the bias will add stability but will not change the bias characteristic of the design.
- **Knits:** Like bias, you do not want to eliminate the stretch, but you want it stable enough for embroidery. Fabrics can be easily embroidered but require a fabric stabilizer to anchor or stabilize the looping of the threads. A fusi-knit is superior for this. The exception would be wanting to fully eliminate stretch in the knit, and in that case, you would apply a fusible woven interfacing, making it no longer a knit.

Heavyweight Fabrics

Dense designs have exceptional results on a stable fabric that can support all the details. Heavier fabrics may be durable enough that they do not require any sort of fabric interfacing, eliminating this step altogether. As discussed on page 29, you should always test the combination of fabric and design to determine what is best.

- **Denim and twill:** A nonstretch denim or twill is usually stable enough that it will not require interfacing to the back of the fabric. Simply add the embroidery stabilizer.
- **Stretch denim and denim-like fabrics:** With the incorporation of stretch fibers, more medium to heavier weight fabrics feature stretch characteristics. The area with stretch should be interfaced to prevent skewing of the embroidery, especially if the embroidery is dense. These types of fabrics also stretch from the tension of the embroidery hoop, so stabilizing the stretch of the fabric is necessary. A medium-weight fusible interfacing will take care of this issue.
- **Canvas:** Embroidery blanks, such as tote bags, flags, and pictures, are often made from a stiff canvas. These items are usually stable enough to omit fabric stabilization. The exception

This wool bag is sewn from a dense and stable fabric and therefore does not need anything to support the fabric.

would be a canvas with an open weave where the grain might skew, but because it is stable, embroidery stabilizer will usually do the trick. Incorporate spray adhesive to attach the embroidery stabilizer.

- **Leather, suedes, and skins:** Leather is different in that it is not a fabric and has no grain. The need to stabilize the fabric is minimal. A heavier hide would be so dense that nothing would be necessary, but a lightweight suede may have some lightweight stretch if pulled tight enough. However, because of the nature of this material, fabric interfacing is not usually necessary and the embroidery stabilizer is sufficient.
- **Upholstery:** Adding embroidery to pillows, curtains, and home décor items is a wonderful way to customize your living space. These fabrics range from dense and stable to medium weight with yarns that may need anchoring. For example, tweeds have yarns that float over other yarns in the fabric structure. Adding a fusible knit will hold them in place so you do not have to worry about them when adding the embroidery.

These examples should get you thinking about how interfacings are added to the fabric and the reasons why you would address this element prior to embroidering. If you are not sure if your fabric needs interfacing, simply stitch a sample, print the sample card, and add your sample to it as a reference for any time you embroider on that fabric. Include any notes of things that worked and did not work. You will start to find you sew a lot of the same types of fabric and project combinations, and this step will be needed less as you develop more knowledge and experience. For extra reference, Chapter 7 is complete with detailed combinations of popular embroidery scenarios.

TIP: Remember that interfacings are used to support the characteristics of the fabric structure only.

CHAPTER 3

Stabilizers and Toppings

Once the characteristics of the fabric or object to be stitched have been addressed and are ready to receive the embroidery, the next step is to select a single layer or combination of embroidery stabilizers to support the design stitches. Some projects utilize a single layer of stabilizer while others have far superior results with a custom selection of layered stabilizers, each with a specific purpose.

What are Stabilizers?

The embroidery stabilizer creates a foundation for the stitches to rest upon. Combined with the fabric in the hoop, the correct stabilizer will eliminate puckering or ripples as a design is being sewn, prevent holes that could potentially show up in the fabric by lack of support, and allow for correct alignment of the design stitches, preventing gaps between the fills. Stabilizers aid in the process of embroidery and for those left in the project after stitching, they will support the design during wear or use of a project.

According to industry leader Oklahoma Embroidery Supply & Design (OESD), most stabilizers are nonwoven material, made in a process where the fibers are smoothed into a single consistent layer. OESD's stabilizers, for example, are equally strong in all directions, so you can hoop in any direction, and there is no grain to match the fabric. For tearaway stabilizers, this nondirectional feature also means that the stabilizer will tear evenly in all directions.

TIP: When selecting a stabilizer, it is essential to look for consistency in the fibers. When you select a brand of stabilizer, hold it up to the light to see if there are any inconsistencies. The lighter areas will provide less support than the darker/thicker areas, which can result in alignment issues.

This array of stabilizers shows a sampling of options for your embroidery design, such as the dress on page 6.

HOW DO YOU SELECT A STABILIZER?

OESD further shared that different stabilizers work with various applications, and many factors go into the selection, such as:

- **Fabric choice:** What is the weight of the fabric? The heavier the fabric, the heavier the stabilizer needed. Two layers of a lighter stabilizer may provide better results than a single heavy layer, especially on a lighter weight fabric.
- **Design density:** How many stitches does the design have over a given area? The denser a design, the more support you will need, which means a heavier stabilizer. A dense design on a lighter weight fabric may stitch better with two layers of lightweight stabilizer rather than a single heavy.
- **Application:** How will the project be hooped during stitching? For some designs, you will hoop only the stabilizer and then affix the fabric over top. This technique is called floating (see page 58).
- **Results:** What do you want the front and back of the design to look like?
- **Other:** Anything unique to your project may affect your selection, such as how you will care for the project. Does the stabilizer need to stay attached to support the stitching or be removed?

Stabilizer selection is a combination of basic selections and descriptions from the product manufacturer, but more importantly, it is based on the knowledge and experience you will develop as your experience in machine embroidery grows. You will start to develop a favorite stabilizer that works best with the type of embroidery and projects you stitch. Use the sample card on page 31 and remember: While there are recommended stabilizers for certain applications, there is no one size that fits all. If you try a recommended combination and it is not giving you the results you desire, then adjust your selections until you determine what works best for your design. Embroidery designers all have their own preferences, and you will too, especially as improvements to current selections and new variations come to the embroidery marketplace.

TYPES OF STABILIZERS

Stabilizers are usually divided into general categories based on how you remove them. These include cutaway, tearaway, wash-away, and heat-away. These stabilizers then have light-, medium-, and heavyweight designations. Within each

(Right to Left) The green fabric is a very delicate fabric with metallic yarn inserts that are unstable. Fusible weft interfacing was added to create a stable surface. This project would not have been possible without this step. Next, a medium cutaway embroidery was attached to the back of the fabric to support the stitching on the pattern pieces. Finally, another layer of lightweight fusible knit interfacing was placed over the entire piece to blend all the embellishments into one allover flat surface for garment assembly. See the finished design on page 6.

category there are numerous options. Do not skimp on quality when it comes to stabilizers.

While it might seem tempting to buy bulks of inexpensive ones online, find a quality brand of stabilizers that will provide consistency and dependable results. Additionally, reputable companies usually have education for their products, further ensuring success for your project. Such a small, but important, part of the embroidery process can be affected by an inferior product. Use the sample card on page 31 to test the stabilizers in a variety of fabric and design combinations. This will help you familiarize yourself with how they perform under different scenarios. You will add to your sample binder and gain some vast experience with your embroidery machine in the process.

Tearaway Stabilizers

Tearaway stabilizer is meant to be temporary and removed after stitching, making it a preferable option for many embroidery projects with a clean outline on the back side of a design. As the design is stitched, the needle punctures the stabilizer for easy removal. A tearaway stabilizer works best on a dense design where the tearing will not stretch or skew the fabric or stabilizer during removal. It is ideal for woven fabrics and comes in a variety of weights.

During removal, it is important not to rip the stabilizer off. Instead, place the project flat on the table with the right side facing down. Support the stitched design by pressing down. With your other hand, gently pull away, starting at one side of the design and working around. This prevents stitching from being pulled and distorted. Some examples of projects that use a tearaway stabilizer include towels, appliqués, buttonholes, bags, and accessories.

Cutaway Stabilizers

Cutaway stabilizer is the most durable and permanent of the stabilizers. It can support those designs with the most stitches and will provide dependable results, preventing stretching in fabrics like knits and those with a flexible or open weave. Cutaways come in a variety of weights, fusible options, and even mesh. If you have a design that is not stitching correctly, changing to a cutaway may just do the trick.

Tearaway easily pulls away from this cotton fabric and moderately dense design.

Cutaway takes a bit more work because you need to carefully trim around the edge of the design.

Cutaways are the best option for knits. When stitching on a knit, the fabric will stretch—even if subtly—thus skewing the design. The fabric may have been anchored with an interfacing, but chances are it still stretches. The cutaway is necessary to provide stability. Have you ever seen a polo shirt or T-shirt with an embroidered logo that did not look right for some reason? Chances are the stabilizer was incorrect, and the fabric stretched.

To remove a cutaway, trim the stabilizer slightly outside the design so you do not cut the fabric or stitches. You will want to leave approximately ¼" (6.35mm) beyond the design, leaving the remaining stabilizer to support the design. Some examples

Stabilizers come on rolls or in precut pieces in a variety of lengths and widths. Most are usually white or black. Topical versions may come in clear or other colors to blend the thread.

STABILIZER SCENARIO

When using a single heavy layer of tearaway stabilizer on a densely stitched design, it can start to perforate and detach during stitching. Even though it is in a hoop, this perforation of the stabilizer will cause issues, such as poor stitching and skewing of the design. The stitches begin to skip, stitch on top of each other, or have gaps between them. If there is too much tension on the thread, it can break; or worse, there is needle breakage, and your project may be ruined. While tearaway may seem quick and convenient, the valued trait is working against you in this scenario.

To counter this, a great technique is to layer different interfacings. The main interfacing used to support the stitches is still tearaway, but by adding a thin layer of cutaway mesh behind the tearaway, this issue is avoided. After stitching, trim away the mesh with fine-point shears (page 28) and then remove the tearaway outside the design. Cutaway is an excellent option for supporting an embroidery design if you want a single layer. An embroidery project is a custom project, and one-size-fits-all may not always be the best. Of course, this is where sampling is key.

of projects using cutaways include T-shirts, knits, children's designs, fabrics with mechanical stretches, or any project where absolute stability is called for.

Wash-Away or Water-Soluble Stabilizers

When a stabilizer is necessary for application but requires no trace left behind afterward, wash-away or water-soluble stabilizers are a wonderful addition to the embroidery studio. Made from starchy materials that dissolve in water after the embroidery is applied, these stabilizers will leave no residue. A water-soluble stabilizer cannot hold as many stitches as a cutaway, but they are useful on lighter fabrics and designs. Additionally, they make ideal toppings for fabrics, such as velveteen, terry cloth, and faux fur, providing a layer for the stitches to be applied to without sinking into the fabric. The fabric simply needs to be washable so the stabilizer can be removed.

Wash-away stabilizers are removed using warm water. For projects with heavyweight single layers or multiple layers, soak in a container with warm water according to the manufacturer's suggested instructions. After it has dissolved, rinse the item well under running water to remove any residue. If the project is stiff after rinsing and drying, then there is a remaining starch residue. Do an

Wash-away allows you to remove the backing to make freestanding items.

additional soak and a solid rinse to remove the final film. Some items like lace may require an iron after soaking to flatten the design. For delicate projects featuring a lightweight layer, a spritz bottle with warm bottle will usually remove the stabilizer.

Projects that pair well with water-soluble stabilizers include bridal veil or tulle materials, sheer fabrics used in garments (like chiffon or organza), freestanding lace, and appliqués.

Heat-Away or Heat-Soluble Stabilizers

Like wash-away stabilizers, heat-away are temporary but use heat to melt away the layer after stitching. No water is necessary, so this is ideal for fabrics and projects that cannot be washed or would spot if using a water removal. This stabilizer is made from heat-activated materials that disappear when heat is applied.

Heat-away is a dry process. To remove a heat-sensitive stabilizer, use a hot dry iron and avoid getting it wet, so do not use steam. Water can cause the stabilizer materials to melt onto your project, causing other issues. Heat around the outer edge of the design with the tip of your iron and then tear away the excess that spans beyond the stitching. During the heating process, it may discolor as it burns up, which is a normal reaction. It is not necessary to press the entire area on the back of the project because you are not applying it like an iron-on stabilizer. Finish with a flat press on the back of the embroidery to remove the rest. After using the dry iron, lightly brush away what is left of the stabilizer; this is a time-efficient process.

Projects that are ideal for a heat-soluble stabilizer include delicate fabrics that water spot, such as silk and velvet, laser-cut or burned designs, and lace. Always test the heat-soluble stabilizer with a sample of your fabric and follow the manufacturer's specialized instructions.

What are Toppings?

Stabilizers affix to the back side of an embroidery project, but some fabrics or projects need support of the stitches on the visible top side. These supportive layers are called toppings and make a dramatic difference in projects that utilize them.

Heat-away is ideal for fabrics that cannot get wet. Upon ironing, the stabilizer disappears.

This embroidery topping supports the threads on the fabric surface.

We have already seen that wash-away can be used as a light topping for some designs, but actual toppings, such as a clear film, create an invisible barrier between the embroidery thread and the nap of the fabric. An example would be a lofty towel with a monogrammed embroidery. Without a topping, the stitching would sink into the pile of the fabric, but a clear topping will support the stitches, so they sit on top of the fabric and create a pristine finish to the design.

To use a topping, place your hooped fabric or object into the embroidery machine, apply all your settings, and find where the center of your design will be located. Cut a piece of topping in a round or rectangular shape slightly larger than your design to be stitched. When you are ready to begin

Stabilizer Quick Reference

DESIGN DENSITY GUIDE

Best for:

- heavy = **heavy** design density
- medium = **medium** design density
- light = **light** design density
- * = **all** design densities

	CUTAWAY						
	Heavy Weight	StabilStick	Medium Weight	PolyMesh	Fusible PolyMesh	Fusible Woven	Heavy Weight
Baby Garments				light – medium	light – medium		
Canvas/Duck Cloth							heavy
Challis/Rayon				light – medium	light – medium	light – medium	
Cotton Fabrics	heavy		medium – heavy			light – medium	heavy
Denim/Jeans	heavy	medium – heavy	medium	light – medium	light – medium	*	
Flannel				medium	medium	light – medium	heavy
Hard-to-Hoop Items (e.g. Collars)		medium – heavy					
Home Dec Fabrics, Tapestries, etc.	heavy	medium – heavy	medium	medium		*	heavy
Freestanding Lace							
Leather/Suede	heavy						heavy
Linen			medium			light – medium	
Organza/Chiffon							
Paper		light					
Polar Fleece			medium	medium	medium		
Sheer Fabrics							
Silk/Satin							heavy
Sweaters				light – medium	light – medium		
Sweatshirts	medium – heavy	medium – heavy	medium	light – medium	light – medium		
Towels (Terry Cloth)							heavy
Towels (Woven Cloth)						light – medium	heavy
T-Shirt/Polo Shirt	heavy	medium – heavy	medium – heavy	light – medium	light – medium		
Velvet/Velveteen/Velour	heavy	medium	medium – heavy	light – medium	light – medium		

TEARAWAY							TOPPING		WASH-AWAY		
Medium Weight	Ultra Clean and Tear	StabilStick	HydroStick	Light Weight	Ultra Clean and Tear Plus	Ultra Clean and Tear Fusible	Heat2Go	StitcH2O	BadgeMaster	AquaMesh	AquaMesh Plus
					*	*		*		🪶–◗	
◗	*	◗	◗	🪶	*	*					
	*			🪶	*	*	🪶–◗			🪶–◗	🪶–◗
◗	*	◗		🪶	*	*		*		🪶–◗	
								*			
◗	*				*	*		*			
		◗	◗		*						🪶
◗	*	◗		🪶	*		*				
									*	*	
◗	*	◗			*		*	*			
	*			🪶	*	*		*			
									◗	🪶–◗	🪶–◗
	🪶			🪶		🪶					
							◗–[weight]	*			
										🪶	🪶
◗	*	◗		🪶	*	*					
							◗–[weight]	*			
							◗–[weight]	*			
◗	*		◗	🪶			◗–[weight]	*		🪶	◗
◗	*	◗		🪶	*	*		*		🪶	
							◗–[weight]	*			
					*			*			

Oklahoma Embroidery Supply & Design (OESD)

stitching, place the topping on top of the hooped fabric. Hold the topping in place (optional: if your machine has a basting feature, you can baste the topping in place around the perimeter of the design), and press start to begin stitching. Begin on a slower stitching speed and monitor it while it creates the outline of the embroidery design. This outline stitch will hold the topping in place. Increase stitching speed and embroider.

After the embroidery is complete and you remove the hoop from the machine, carefully peel away the topping that is sticking out from the outer edge of the design. The stitches of the design will cover the rest of the topping, but anything sticking out can be carefully peeled away. Because some of the toppings are heat-sensitive, if there are tiny areas of a design where you cannot peel away, such as in the middle of a letter, take the tip of your iron and melt away the excess. Of course, do a test first to make sure it will not spot your project and that the topping will disintegrate away.

Projects that require a topping to support the visible face of the embroidery include towels, fleece, stuffed animals, velvet, and any material that has a nap or texture where the stitching might sink down into it.

Specialty Stabilizers

Beyond the core types of stabilizers, there are numerous options with very specialized use in embroidery. Logo hats, for example, use puffy foam as a topping. When stitched, the foam creates a ridge that sits away from the item being sewn for depth and definition. More examples include gentle backings that provide a soft layer next to the skin; fiber foam stabilizers that support freestanding projects like ornaments, houses, and toys; adhesive templates that can be printed on prior to stitching; and many more. New stabilizers and toppings are continually brought to the embroidery market, adding to the enjoyment and possibilities of sewers everywhere.

With any material, the embroidery enthusiast will need to navigate all the marketing to determine what is good, dependable quality versus mass-produced, poor-quality options sold online. Shop from reputable brands and dealers, reference your favorite brands for their specific uses and guidelines, recognize one size does not fit all, and remember that recommended options may not always work for what you are doing. Stabilizers are a key element of successful embroidery. Take some time to practice; test and experiment to determine what works best on your machine and projects. Chapter 7 features popular scenarios in embroidery and suggests stabilizers for them.

Now that we understand how stabilizers and toppings support embroidery stitching to look their best, there are just a few more ingredients to the formula for a successful embroidery project.

A foam topping is good for fonts and thick monograms.

This foam is making the lettering pop on the railroad-themed hat.

CHAPTER 4

Size, Placement, and Marking

There are two sizes to consider when applying machine embroidery: the size of the actual embroidery design to be stitched and the size of the embroidery hoop. All embroidery machines have a maximum stitching area size, and it is different from one model or brand to another. You will want to take into consideration the size of the embroidery design and determine if it will fit into the parameters of your machine. Using the smallest hoop possible will support the design best while eliminating any waste of fabric or stabilizers. It is also important to know the size of your design and how it fits into the area on the project you will embroider.

To better understand the combination of design and hoop size, you will need the following information:

1. **Design selection.** Your machine has a maximum size of design it can stitch. Make sure any embroidery design you purchase is no larger than your machine's largest capabilities. If your design is slightly larger than your hoop or stitching area, you have the option to reduce the size; however, there are limits as to how much you can reduce a design before it becomes too dense. For best results, reducing or increasing no more than 10 percent is recommended for best quality. Reference editing options on 26. Many designs are available in assorted sizes to fit most popular hoop sizes. If your selected design is not available to fit your machine or it is not editable, select an alternate from the endless options available. Additionally, having an alternate design as a backup is a good workroom tip for any project.
2. **Machine size and cost.** When selecting an embroidery machine, you will want to ask yourself what types of projects and sizes you will be embroidering. Are your projects smaller in size and scope? Are they in-the-hoop projects or smaller things like accessories? Will you need larger hoops for quilt blocks, continuous patterns, and overall larger designs and layouts? Larger hoops and machine features will cost more, so this is an important consideration when planning an embroidery budget.
3. **Measurement units.** Hoops and embroidery designs are measured in millimeters or inches. If you have a preference, use a conversion chart to find what the conversion would be. For example, a design that measures 4.02" x 5.69" would equal 102.11 x 144.53mm. Embroidery machines and many design software have the option to select how you view the design in either the millimeters or inches. Knowing this will help you make the correct size selection to match your machine's capabilities. We will learn more about hooping techniques in Chapter 5.

HOOP SIZE MEASUREMENTS

INCHES	MM
4 x 4	100 x 100
5 x 5	120 x 120
5 x 7	130 x 180
6 x 10	160 x 260
8 x 8	200 x 200
8 x 12	200 x 300
8 x 14	200 x 360
9.5 x 14	240 x 360

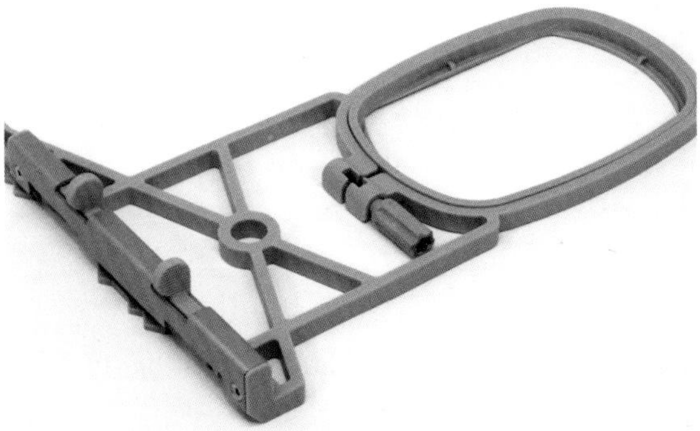

This small hoop has a stitching area of 2" x 2.8" (50.8 x 71.12mm) and is ideal for small embroidery designs, children's clothing, sleeves, and free-arm stitching.

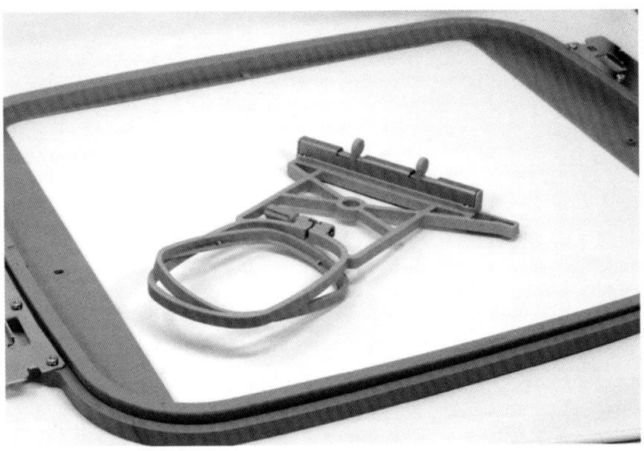

Surrounding the small hoop is a maxi hoop with a 14" x 14" (355.6 x 355.6mm) stitching area, ideal for border embroidery and large design.

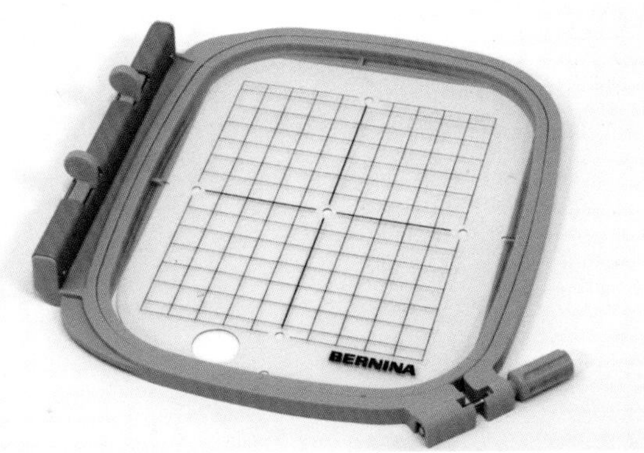

Some embroidery hoops come with a coordinating template to assist in sizing and placement of the embroidery design.

4. **Stitching area.** Hoop size does not always equal stitching area. The actual stitching area of a hoop may be smaller than the measurement listed in the hoop. For example, a 4" x 4" (101.6 x 101.6mm) hoop may have a maximum stitching area of 3.85" x 3.85" (97.79 x 97.79mm). This is because the needle and foot need space to move, thus reducing the total stitching area in the open portion of the hoop. Make sure to select or size your design to the *stitching area* and not the hoop size.
5. **Hoop template.** Embroidery hoops usually come with a translucent plastic template that is placed inside the hoop. If you do not have this for your hoop, you could easily trace one on cardstock or make a clear template from a vellum paper. This template clearly illustrates the actual stitching area of the individual hoop and is an effective tool for precise design placement and sizing. It is also helpful in transferring the size and area of the design to the item being stitched for even more accurate placement.
6. **Stitch outline.** To test where the boundary of the stitches will be on your project, use the stitch outline function. The machine will simply outline the area where the design will be located by moving around the perimeter, helping you to visualize the stitching area when setting up your design in the embroidery machine. Many machines have a basting feature as well. The machine will baste a square perimeter around the area where the design will fall. Never skip this step. It is one last check and balance for correct stitching, size, and placement. Note: Higher-end machines have things like lasers and other features to further aid in precision placement. From a simple template to laser outline, these tools are a part of the process in preparing your project to receive the stitching.
7. **Duplicates for efficiency.** Copy and paste to make duplicates and stitch multiples of a design using a larger hoop. This will help you save time by making many designs in one hooping. With a little planning of the design size and hoop size, you can determine how many will fit into the machine's largest hoop and make multiple stitching very efficient.

Stitch Count and Density

Designs include a total stitch count or number of individual stitches that also affects their application and the types of projects they are best suited for. The higher the number of stitches, the longer it takes for the machine to stitch it out. How these stitches present themselves can look different from one design to another: the stitches may be close together in a very compact area or spaced out over a larger area.

The density of a design is simply how many stitches are in an area of measure and how close or spread apart they are. Although a large, open design may have more stitches than a small motif, the smaller design might be denser with stitches in a smaller area. Additionally, a large design like lace may have lots of stitched details and embroidery elements, making it not only dense with a high stitch count but also larger in scope.

Careful consideration should be taken to combine the right density of a design with your fabric or project. A dense (high stitch count) design on delicate fabric will easily collapse, tear, or skew because the fabric does not provide enough support. It would be more effective to select a less dense design for a fine fabric or create an appliqué that can be affixed to the delicate fabric (see page 72) rather than stitching directly onto the lighter fabric. Some embroidery designs feature a combination of high stitch count areas while other parts of the design have fewer stitches. Before assigning a particular design to your project, you would want to take the density into consideration as well as what stabilizers would be necessary to balance the differences before you begin stitching. Designs all vary. The denser the design, the sturdier stabilizer and fabric needed to support the stitches. Review stabilizer tips in Chapter 3.

If you are into digitizing your own embroidery, be mindful of layering too many stitches on each other or in the same area. Stitching issues arise when too many stitches land on top of each other. Thread breakage and other issues may arise in the stitching. Therefore, good digitizers and embroidery designs will not place lots of stitches on top of each other when creating the pattern.

When selecting and pairing a design with a project, it is important to remember that not all designs work with all types of garments, fabrics, or objects. Evaluate the size and weight of the project with the scale, size, and density of the embroidery design for best results; if you are not sure, test a sample to determine the results.

(Left) This is a good example of a design that has high density. It needs to be stitched on a stable fabric that can support it, and it would use a cutaway stabilizer.

(Right) This is a low-density design. It has open edges and space between the leaves, making it ideal for lighter projects or as a freestanding design.

Design Placement and Alignment

After choosing your embroidery design and stabilizer, set up the stitching surface for accurate placement. Evaluate the project and avoid elements that may prevent embroidery like thick seams or a zipper. You may need to place the design around these things or another area on the project. There is no lack of special tools available in the marketplace today to aid in placement of embroidery designs. You may find that you have a favorite alignment tool that may also aid in efficiency, and there is nothing wrong with these tools. For any specialty tool, research specific tutorials and demonstrations from the product's manufacturer.

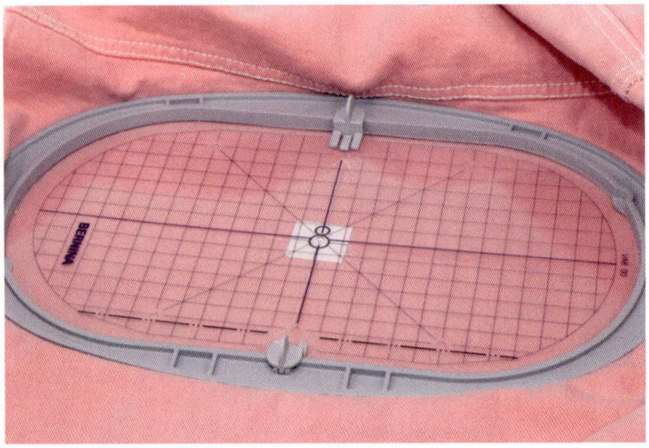

If your hoop has the companion clear template, use it to double check placement prior to stitching.

STEPS TO ACHIEVE CORRECT PLACEMENT

For this tutorial, we are covering the basics that work for any scenario, and in all practicality, there is no magic tool or formula. Before all these tools were available, placement accuracy started by using one practical tool in your sewing room: a ruler. However, nothing is worse than finishing an embroidery only to find out it is in the wrong location, so let us look at some general guidelines that ensure placement success every time.

As a reminder, you will use the smallest hoop for the design and area being stitched, making sure they will both fit the embroidery project. For example, embroidery on a shirt sleeve will require a smaller hoop and design due to the obvious size constraints, whereas a large garment can utilize a larger design and hoop. These decisions should be made prior to alignment.

1. Center marking placement. The key to design placement begins by matching the center of the embroidery design with the center of the area you are to embroider. Clearly mark your project exactly where you want the center of the design to be placed (see Marking Tips on page 54).

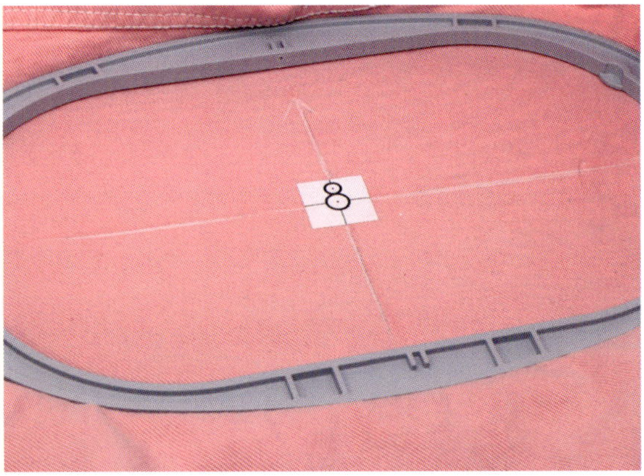

2. Horizontal and vertical placement image. To align the vertical and then horizontal orientation, make sure the top of the embroidery design is placed facing the upward direction of your project along with the left and right sides. Not all embroidery designs are symmetrical left and right or from top to bottom, so these placement areas are important.

3. Placement marking on a design. Add the visible marking lines or notations to the project being stitched. Not all projects need actual marking lines, so you will need to determine when it is necessary:

3a. If you are adding embroidery to a square pillow form and the embroidery design is a symmetrical design, then a small mark indicating the center of the project will be sufficient. Simply center the project in the hoop and begin stitching.

3b. Items, such as a jacket, stuffed animal, or even a T-shirt, that require precise placement may need some tangible guidelines to line up the design. Select a method of marking that is best for your fabric or item.

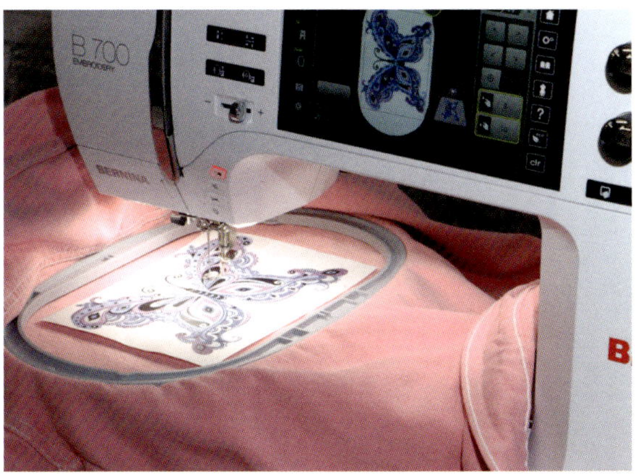

4. Directional buttons on the machine. Join the fabric to the hoop and secure placement during the process of hooping (see Chapter 5). Attach the hooped item to the machine. When designs are not hooped directly in the center, use the directional buttons to aid in placement. This allows you to move the center of the design up, down, left, right, and diagonally. Some machines even have laser tools that further simplify the process. With careful plotting of the design, your embroidery will be perfect every time.

OPTIONAL PAPER EMBROIDERY DESIGN TEMPLATE

Using a template of the actual embroidery design is an easy, inexpensive, and accurate tool to visualize the design on your project being stitched. There is really no guesswork because you can see it on the stitching surface. To make a paper template:

1. **Paper template.** Print off the template for your embroidery design in the actual size, if provided, and cut around it as if a paper copy of the design. If you do not have a template, try printing an image of the design instead. Increase or decrease the printable size by adjusting it in the print settings screen.
2. **Visualize.** Check the measurements to ensure they align with your embroidery design and stitching area. Place the paper template on the embroidery surface to visualize how it works on the project and transfer any placement markings (see page 54).

Although certain machines are equipped with advanced features, such as laser placement lines and integrated cameras, many models do not include these capabilities. However, as your embroidery skills develop and you become more adept with recent technology, these flat representations can effectively replace traditional templates. Some embroidery professionals continue to use precise templates in lieu of the technology features.

Print out a paper template of the design in color and use it as a last way to check placement of the design before stitching.

Stitch out an embroidery design to use as a template. This is more accurate than your embroidery machine screen, and you can clearly see how it will look on the project.

OPTIONAL STITCH SAMPLE TEMPLATE

This is a go-to tool for even more precise placement. Stitch out a sample of the embroidery design, and once complete, trim around the outside of the design. Use it as a realistic example of the design for placement.

Although not necessary for a design, this is extremely useful when stitching duplicates of a pattern, such as for making fabric, and allows you to place the design in various angles to nest them in specific ways and move around on the fabric or project in ways the computer screen cannot replicate. (This is my favorite method for creating embroidery fabric or large panels for clothing.)

Once you find a technique that works for you—whether it's the basic placement, a paper template, or a stitched template—make notes or a sample card as a reference for the next time you create the same project or one similar.

Common Embroidery Locations

There are numerous embroidery placement rulers, tools, charts, and gadgets for enhancing and marking the location of embroideries on a variety of projects. While most have similar guidelines and recommendations, it is okay to modify these locations as needed according to the size and shape of your customized project. Here is a collection of commonly suggested positions that are all based on vertical and horizontal orientation. Shift any design up, down, left, or right based on the size of embroidery, weight of the project, placement of thick seams or trims to avoid, and what ultimately looks best.

TOWELS

- **Hand towel:** 2" (5.08cm) up from the bottom hem and centered
- **Wash cloth:** 2" (5.08cm) up from the bottom and centered, or 1" (2.54cm) from the corner when monogramming
- **Bath towel:** 2"–4" (5.08–10.16cm) up from the bottom hem and centered, or 2" (5.08cm) above the woven binding

Towels are typically embroidered along the edge.

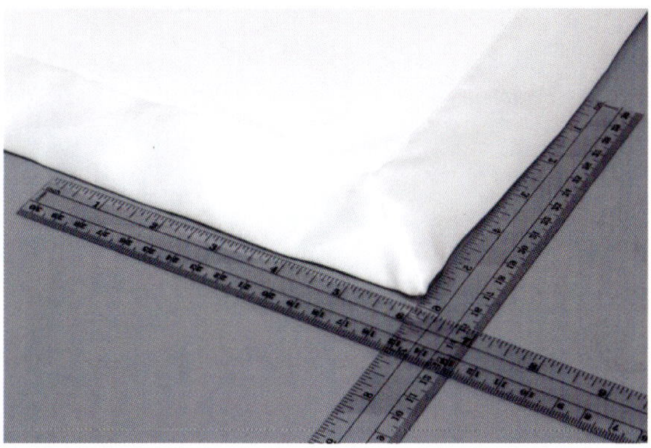

Blankets are typically embroidered at the corner.

HOME ITEMS

- **Pillowcase:** Centered using horizontal and vertical measurements
- **Cloth napkin:** 2" (5.08cm) up from the bottom hem and centered, or 1" (2.54cm) from the corner when monogramming
- **Blanket:** 3"–4" (7.62–10.16cm) from the bottom-left or -right corner

KIDS ITEMS

- **Onesie:** 2"–4" (5.08–10.16cm) down from the center front and centered
- **Bib:** Centered on the item; for extra-long bibs, 2"–4" (5.08–10.16cm) down from the center front and centered
- **Blanket:** 3"–4" (7.62–10.16cm) from the bottom-left or -right corner

CLOTHING

- **T-shirt:** 4"–6" (10.16–15.24cm) down from the center front of the neckline and centered; adjust based on rounded or V-neck styles
- **Polo shirt:** 7"–9" (17.78–22.86cm) down from the middle of the shoulder and 3"–6" (7.62–15.24cm) from the middle of the shirt

MARKING FROM THE CORNER

For embroidery on rectangular items where the location is placed according to the left or right edge, starting at the corner, measure along one edge and up the other. Make sure they are equidistant.

Multiple rulers come in handy when finding the exact center.

Onesies are typically embroidered at the center, like a shirt.

- **Shirt with pocket:** Follow T-shirt and polo shirt guidelines to place on the pocket or just above the pocket. Note: The pocket may need to be removed and then reapplied after stitching.
- **Jacket:** 7"–9" (17.78–22.86cm) down from the middle of the shoulder
- **Shirt cuff:** On the top of the wrist slightly toward the front. For best placement, measure on the wearer or fold the sleeve in half and place it 1" (2.54cm) toward the front from the folded edge.
- **Sleeve:** For a single motif to fall on the arm, place the embroidery slightly toward the front so it is visible from the front. For best placement, follow the guidelines for marking a pattern piece (page 54).
- **Collar point:** Place according to the pattern piece. Use the mirror image feature in the machine for a left and right view.

Shirts are typically embroidered at the chest.

Embroidery on a necktie is placed based on what will be visible.

ACCESSORIES

- **Handkerchief:** ½"–1" (1.27–2.54cm) from the bottom-right corner (usually tiny designs)
- **Necktie:** 2" (5.08cm) up from the point of the tie and centered. If wearing a vest, measure with the vest on and raise the placement so it is visible on the wearer.
- **Cap and beanie:** Centered on the front band

Marking and Marking Tools

The embroidery marking tool is used to place an actual marking or outline of the embroidery design on the item being stitched. When the hooped project is placed under the embroidery machine, the stitching should line up exactly to the markings, resulting in flawless placement of the design. These tools include things like adhesive dots to a variety of pins and chalk, all of which may be temporary or permanent. Some have specific uses, such as the adhesive dots for marking the center, whereas other marking tools, such as a transfer pen, can be used to mark a variety of reference lines. At minimum, they are used to mark the center of the design on the project because this is where the embroidery will start in the machine.

When selecting your marking tools, read all manufacturers' guidelines for removal where applicable. Do a test on a sample, either in a small corner of the fabric or inside the item stitched if there is any concern that the marking may be visible after embroidery. Marking pens and chalk are the most popular but may leave residue on a silk fabric, whereas an adhesive dot may be sufficient for a pillow.

TYPES OF MARKING TOOLS

- **Adhesive dots:** Temporary sticky-backed paper dots with a light adhesive that are used to mark the center of a design.
- **Chalk:** Tailor's chalk is ideal for marking most clothing items. It is meant for natural fibers and will beautifully iron away; however, it will leave a residue on manufactured fibers like polyester, so it is best to limit marking to the center where it will be stitched over. Tailor's chalk is available in a variety of colors, but the chemical composition

is different for each, so even though they are supposed to be heat-away, many leave a mark. Test before use.

- **Water-soluble marking pen:** Temporary and easily removed with damp cloth or cotton swab, these are great for precision with the ultra-fine point. Make sure the fabric won't water spot when removed.
- **Heat-soluble marking pen:** This marking tool is temporary and easily removed by applying heat from a light iron, and it is equally great for precision with the ultra-fine point. Ensure that the iron's temperature matches the requirements of the fabric with which you are working.
- **Iron-on transfer pencil:** By placing tracing or transfer paper over the embroidery design, you may trace the design from the sample template with this pencil. The tracing is placed on the embroidery area and ironed on to transfer it. This pencil can also be used to outline the entire stitching area, which is especially useful when creating a continuous pattern.
- **Graphite pencil:** While not an embroidery-specific marking tool, a readily available and simple #2 pencil with a fine point is often ideal for marking design placement, and it is one of my favorites. The marking will not erase, but it also will not bleed or stain the fabric; it does not require any special application; and a lightly drawn marking is easily hidden under any stitching. The key is to press lightly.
- **Basting:** Though this is an application that may take a little longer, basting is a precision way to get a mark that will not transfer onto the fabric via chemical transfer. This is the best option for fine, delicate fabrics that may shift around during the hooping process. The basted marking may run strategically on a particular thread line and is a smart tool when working with patterned fabrics like stripes, which has many color options for perfect blending. By using a fine, easily concealed thread, any basting not covered by stitching can be quickly removed by snipping the thread.
- **Rulers and plastic templates:** A ruler does not place the actual mark on the project but is necessary for measuring the areas on the project in preparation for receiving the marking. You probably have a variety of rulers in your sewing room that will serve this purpose, but there are

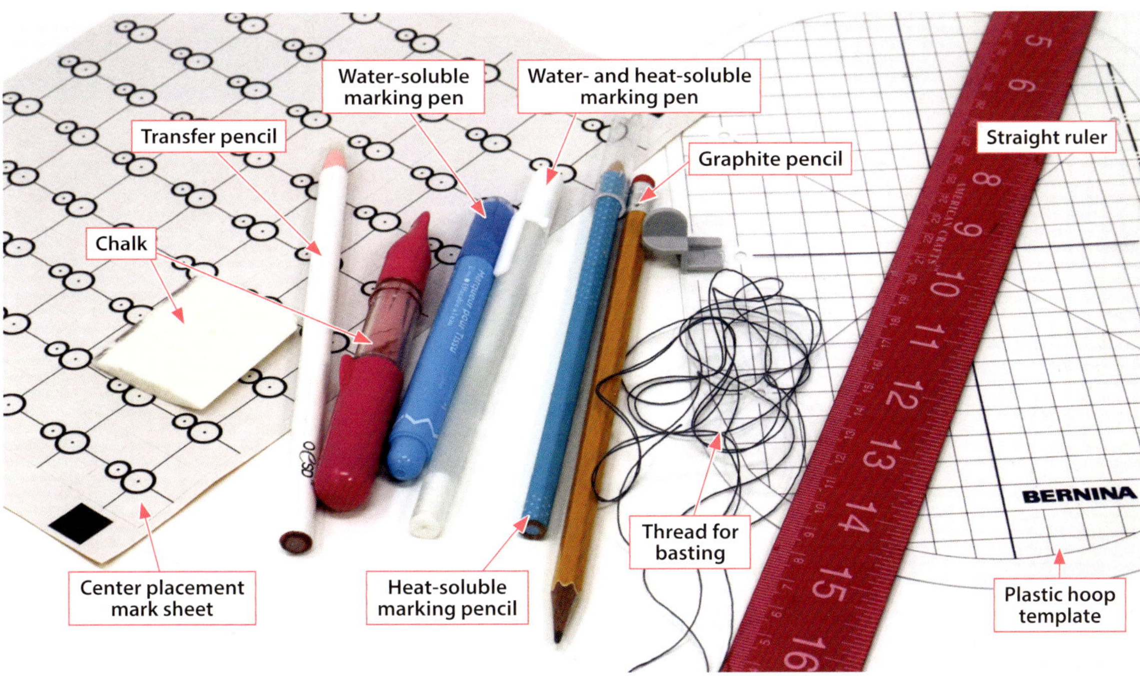

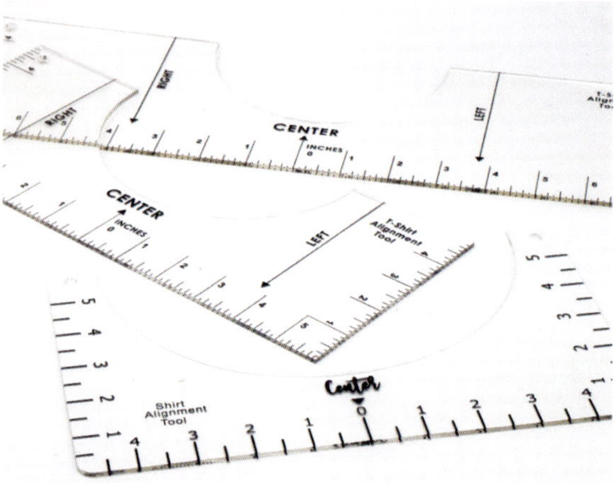

There are a variety of embroidery rulers available, including for design placement on T-shirts as shown here.

many embroidery-specific rulers along with measuring tools developed for embroidery.

MARKING TIPS

1. **Test sample.** When stitching multiples of the same design, create a test sample of the design, thread, fabric, and stabilizer combination. Cut around the design close to the stitching—similar to making an appliqué. This will be used as a template.
2. **Mark the center of the design.** This can be done at the completion of the sample stitch-out since the needle will default back to the beginning and center of the design. Mark there before removing from the embroidery machine, mark the center of the design by referencing the information provided with the design, or fold the design into quarters to find the center. The second and third options may be less accurate.
3. **Position.** Place the stitched template on the fabric and position or rotate tiny amounts for precision placement. Use the marking tool to transfer over the center of the design, at minimum, or completely outline the design.
4. **Stitching.** When placing the hoop in the machine, leave the stitched template sample while setting up the machine. Once it all lines up, remove the template and begin stitching.

A stitch sample was made to test the visual appeal and placement of the design.

Rose appliqués were added, illustrating the possible layout and checking the size pairing between the designs. See this design on page 77.

CHAPTER 5

Hooping Techniques

To ensure a firm surface for embroidery stitches, it is necessary to use an embroidery hoop to keep the item or fabric taut. The traditional method joins the stabilizer to the project between the hoops as one unit, with one of the hoop pieces touching and supporting the fabric and the other supporting the stabilizer. Modifications of this method include floating work with a variety of projects for easy and efficient stitching. Prehooping steps include techniques we have covered, such as stabilized fabric, stabilizer for the embroidery design, marked placement lines on the surface of the project, a design that fits the hoop and embroidery area size, and a density that works with the project. Needle and thread options are addressed in Chapter 6 as the final selections prior to stitching.

Hoop Types and Companion Tools

- **Rectangle hoops:** The most common hoop shape that comes with the embroidery machine is the rectangle. It is available in small sizes for tiny details to large hoops big enough to cover the back of a jacket. On larger hoops, the longer edges may provide less tension than the shorter edges. Use hoop tape to provide consistent support around the entire hoop edge.
- **Round or rounded-edge hoops:** The circular or rounded shape provides the benefit of even

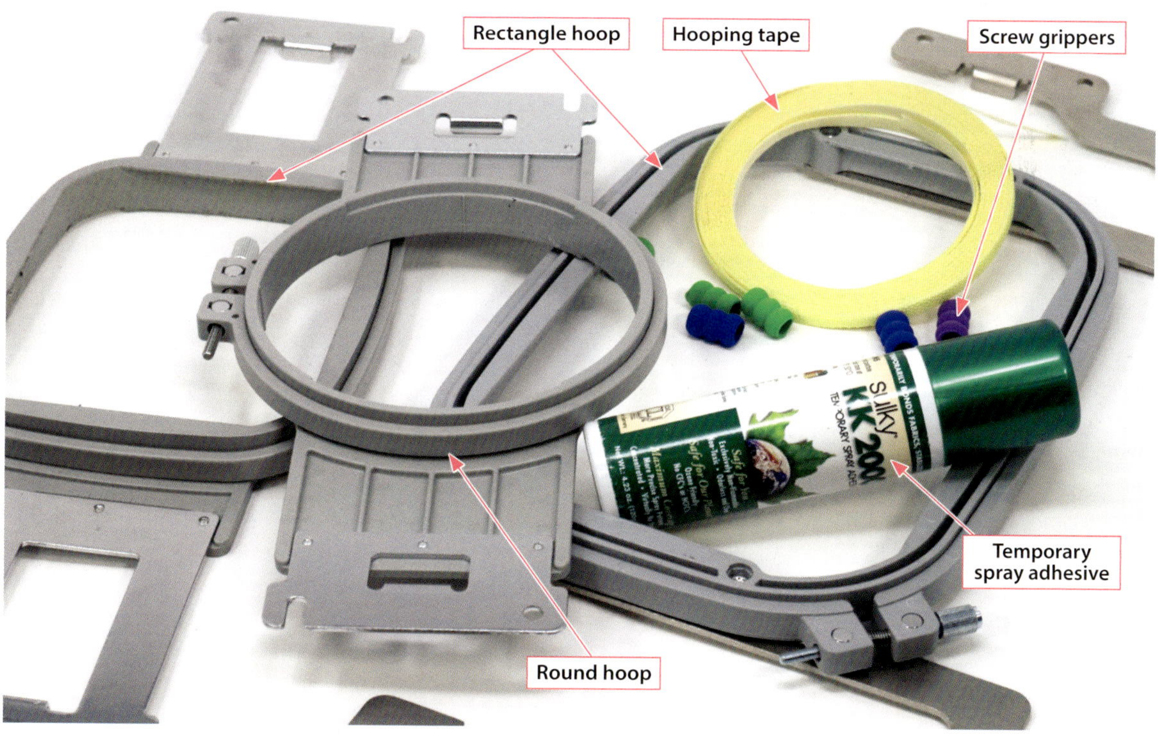

Having a hoop that is just slightly larger than your design will offer the best overall support for stitching.

tension around the entire hooped area of the project. These are ideal for clothing and often used on hard-to-hoop areas like stuffed animals where the squared shape is difficult to fit. If your machine has a round hoop, it is worth the investment.

- **Magnetic hoops:** Like the round hoop, a magnetic hoop offers consistent tension around the entire rim, and it is easy to use. It eliminates the need to adjust the outer ring and screw since it will automatically adjust for the thickness of a project.
- **Multiple hoops:** When stitching multiples of the same item, a duplicate hoop helps you with efficiency. Once the current item finishes stitching, you can get the next piece ready so the machine can start working right away.
- **Specialty hoops:** There are all sorts of specialty tools and hoops to use as you grow your machine embroidery interests and skills. To embroider hats, for example, you will need a hat-specific hoop. Bag hoops come in a variety of sizes, and hooping stations are beneficial for efficiency in hooping and production.
- **Temporary spray adhesive:** This bonding agent works alongside marking and hooping tools. When sprayed onto the stabilizer, it allows you to attach your project before stitching. It dissolves after a brief time and allows you to reposition the fabric before stitching. Hold it far enough away from the design to avoid large drops and use a thin layer. For silk or delicate fabrics, evaluate the spray prior to use to test for stain or residue. Spray adhesive is a great tool for stabilizers that do not have an adhesive property, and it is good for holding layers of fabric together.
- **Hoop tape:** This tape is a thin, temporary adhesive applied to the part of the hoop rim that touches the fabric. Measuring around ¼" (6.35mm), it comes on a roll and is easy to apply. It lasts for multiple hooping while holding the fabric tight to eliminate slippage.
- **Safety pins:** These may be used in hooping to secure copious amounts of fabric, blankets, or clothing that fall outside the hooped area by rolling or folding them. It is important to note you cannot embroider over a pin. The needle is sure to break, and that could be detrimental to the function of your machine if hit during stitching. Keep pins outside of the hooped area.
- **Clamps and hoop clips:** Used in the same way as a safety pin, the embroidery-specific clamp or clip controls large areas outside of the hooping surface to prevent any unintentional drag or pull on the moving embroidery surface.
- **Screw grippers:** These rubber grips fit over the screw on an embroidery hoop to aid in tightening and loosening during the hooping process.

How to Properly Hoop Your Design

In the traditional hooping method, fabric and stabilizer are hooped together as one unit into the embroidery hoop. Use the smallest hoop possible. Work on a flat surface with the embroidery surface marked for stitching following the tips on page 54. Proper hooping will determine the success of your embroidery project.

I suggest practicing the same design a few times to familiarize yourself with the steps for hooping a project.

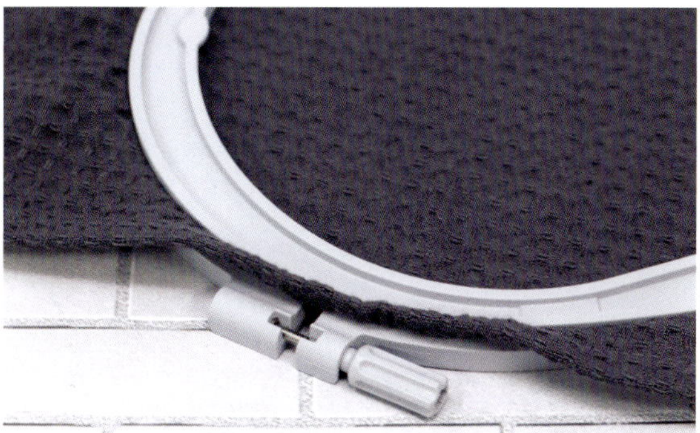

1. Prep the hoop. Loosen the hoop screw so there is just enough space between the outer and inner hoop for the fabric to sandwich between. Excess space is not necessary, but equally, do not force the item between the hoop layers if it does not easily pop in. Take the fabric out and separate the outer and inner hoop.

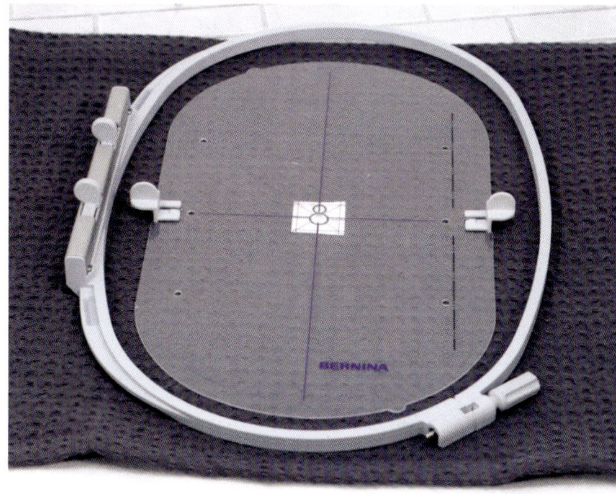

2. Lay the fabric on a flat surface. Make sure there are no wrinkles or bumps. Place the outer hoop on top, positioning the center of your project in the center of the hoop. Use the hoop's reference points or its template to position accurately. Mark the center and remove the hoop.

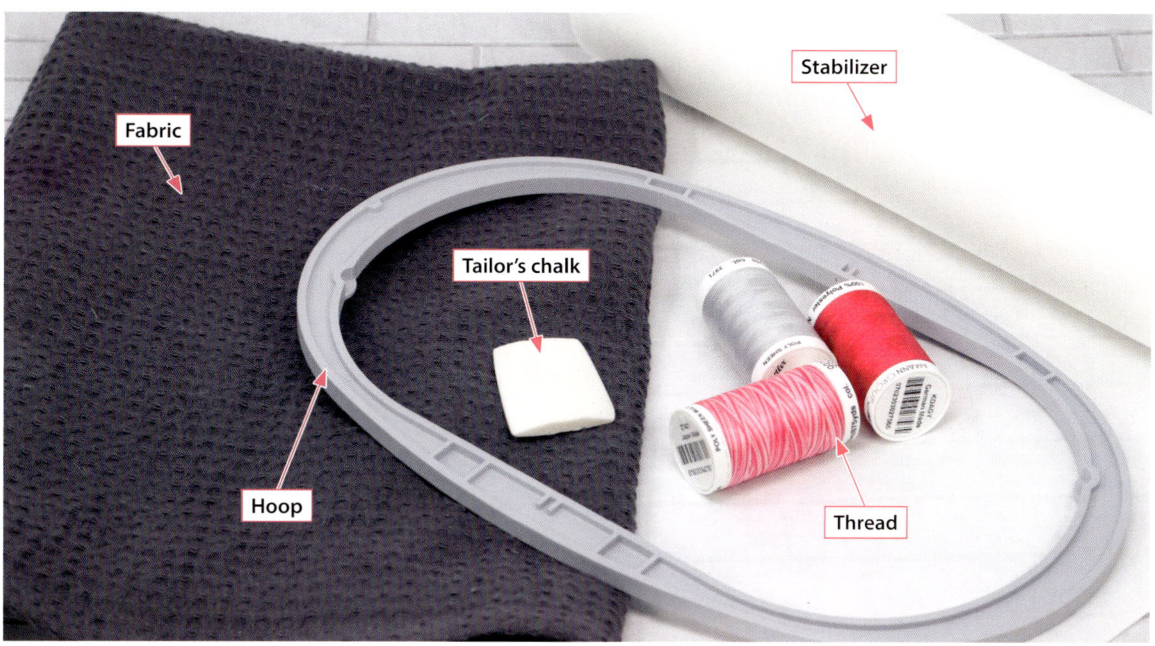

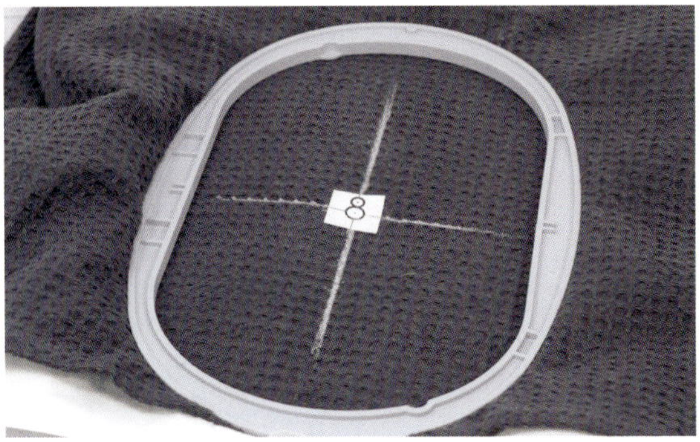

3. Lay the stabilizer and project over the outer hoop. Place the inner hoop on top of the fabric. Line up the reference lines of the hoop with the embroidery placement lines on the project. With even and firm pressure, press in place. If you must force the hoop, stop and loosen the screw a bit until you can press in place easily. Smooth the fabric and pull from the edges gently to tighten up the fabric if necessary.

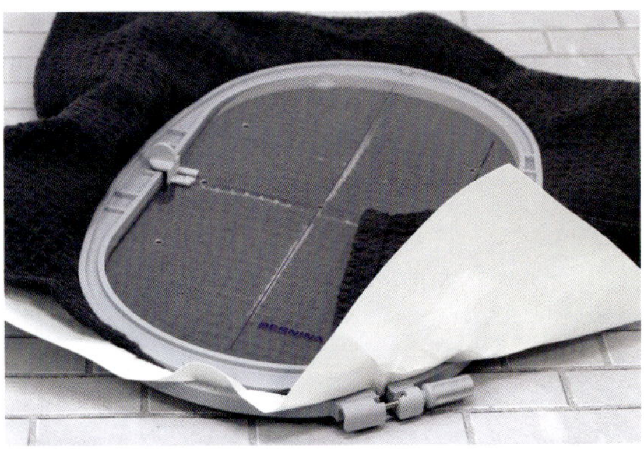

4. Lightly tighten the screw. It should be snug but not overly tight. The fabric should be flat but not pulling tight in the hoop. There should be a scant amount of give to the fabric, which prevents stretching. If it is too tight, the fabric will distort and pucker after removing it from the hoop, and the embroidery will not lay as nicely.

TIP: Do not overtighten either manually or with a screwdriver. This damages the hoop and leaves marks on material.

5. Time to stitch. Make sure everything looks correct on the top and bottom of the hoop, insert into the machine, and watch your design come to life.

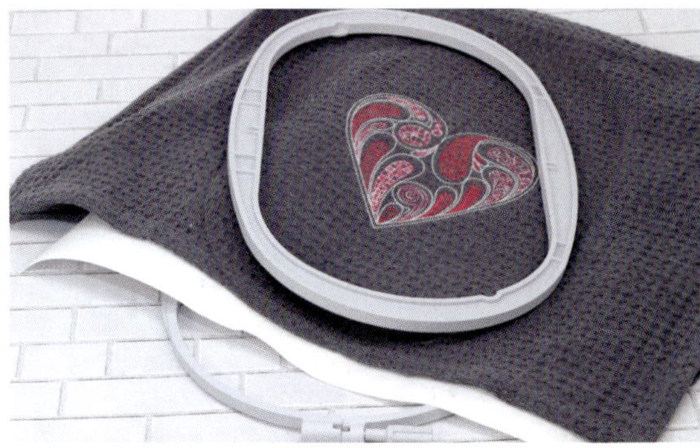

6. Carefully remove the hoop. Loosen the screw and remove your project. For nonpermanent stabilizers, remove according to the type of stabilizer.

Floating Over the Hoop

Floating is a gift to machine embroiderers when used correctly. Although hooping your entire project ensures an optimal stitching surface, floating refers to positioning only the stabilizer inside the hoop without securing the item you want to embroider. It is not for every project, such as precision designs or matching patterns, but is ideal for bulky items, such as a lofty towel, a delicate fabric that you do not want to stretch or damage from the hooping process, something too small to hoop, or an item that is difficult to hoop like a bag. Sticky tearaway stabilizers pair well with the floating technique and are an alternate to spray adhesive. Both have a glue element. If your needle becomes tacky, wipe it with rubbing alcohol.

The metallic fabric of this topper adds another design element to this embroidered project.

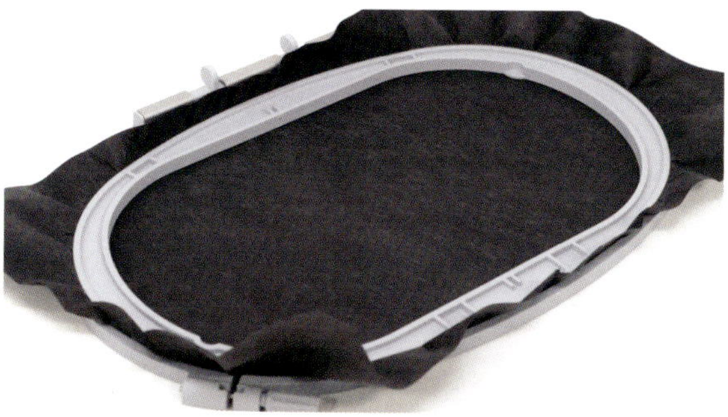

1. Hoop the stabilizer without the project. Mark the center of the hoop and the placement lines for the corresponding embroidery with a pencil. Self-adhesive stabilizers with a peel-away backing are made for this type of hooping.

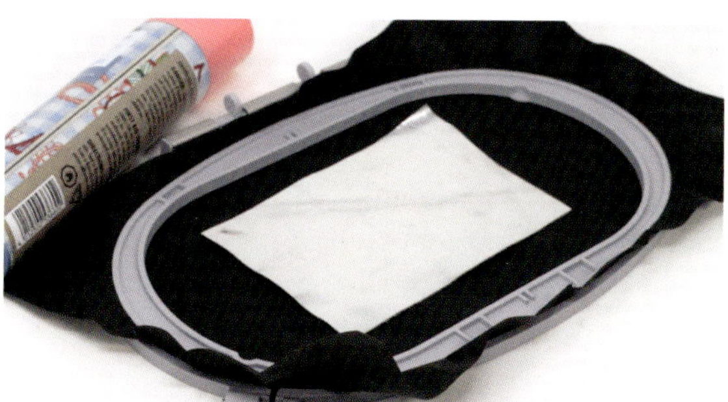

2. Apply spray adhesive to the hoop. Only spray if not using a self-adhesive stabilizer. For fine garments or fabrics, it may be necessary to baste the item to the stabilizer instead of using the adhesive.

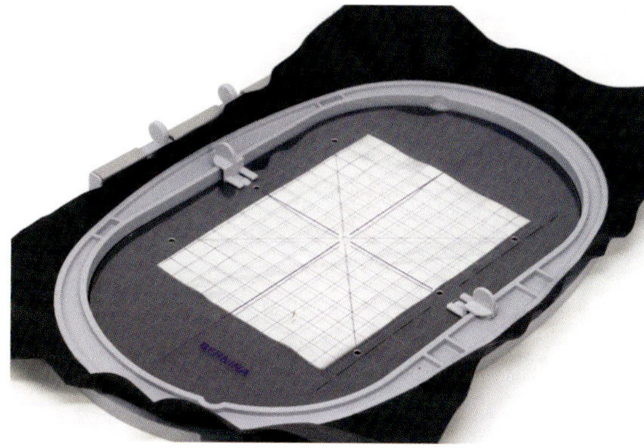

3. Position the fabric over the hooped stabilizer. Line up the center of the design with the center of the hoop. Match the center, horizontal, and vertical areas. Gently press the layers together, covering the entire surface.

4. Carefully place in the embroidery machine for stitching. Use hoop clips, clamps, or safety pins to hold any area not being embroidered out of the way during stitching.

CHAPTER 6

Needles and Threads

Selecting an embroidery thread for machine embroidery is one of the most delightful steps in the process. Designed exclusively for embroidery applications, these threads offer an extensive range of colors and types to accommodate any project or style preference. A wide range of fiber types are suitable for use in embroidery, including polyester, cotton, silk, and rayon; rayon and polyester are the most popular.

Embroidery threads are especially beautiful to look at with all the vibrant colors. Unlike 3-ply sewing thread, embroidery thread is 2-ply, providing a smooth finish and sheen to the embroidery design. The sheen or matte finish of the thread will determine how the final design looks when stitched out. For best results, you will want to pair your thread with the correct needle, pay attention to the characteristics of fiber styles, and follow any particular care considerations.

Types of Embroidery Thread

RAYON THREAD

Rayon is considered a natural fiber because it comes from a naturally occurring cellulose fiber derived from wood pulp that is dissolved and made into rayon fibers. With a high-gloss finish, rayon embroidery thread is soft and has the highest natural shine of all the embroidery threads. Rayon does weaken when wet, is sensitive to heat, and is less colorfast when in contact with chemicals like bleach or other cleaners.

Projects that are best for rayon might include lighter fabrics, home décor where the embroidery is visual only, and items that will not obtain heavy usage or frequent wash and care. Rayon would not be the best choice for a T-shirt or heavy blanket, for example, because of the high wear and care needs.

POLYESTER THREAD

Mettler Thread

Polyester is a synthetic, manufactured fiber derived from a chemical solution that is spun into long fiber lengths. These long fibers are extremely durable, breakage resistant, and colorfast. Polyester is also heat resistant and chemical resistant.

Mettler's POLY SHEEN® thread is often referred to as a "hero" among the brand's sewing threads. They say, "Its properties are particularly important on heavily strained textiles, such as sports and leisure wear, denim, terry cloth, children's, leather, and work wear. The secret of its versatility lies in its composition: the trilobal filament cross section of the sewing thread ensures a larger surface and thus a higher light reflection than with conventional embroidery and decorative sewing threads. The outcome is a vibrant, glossy finish that even after bleaching with chlorine remains for years."

COTTON THREAD

Mettler Thread

Cotton fiber thread provides a matte finish for a softer look on projects like heirloom sewing, handkerchiefs, lacework, costumes, quilting, and historical reproductions where a more authentic look is desired. Colorfastness is an important consideration when using cotton. Cotton thread goes through a mercerization process that makes it strong and heat resistant and reduces shrinkage. Cotton does have the potential to shrink with excessive hot water or steam. It is best to wash in cool water and line dry; or use a delicate and cool cycle in the dryer and steam lightly when pressing. Cotton fibers will provide a beautiful natural look to your embroidery and last a long time with a little consideration to the care for this fiber.

VARIEGATED THREAD

Mettler Thread

Variegated threads are created with more than one color on a single strand of thread. Monochromatic spools feature variations of the same color, creating an ombre effect when stitching, while multicolor spools offer an array from coordinating color palettes to a full rainbow effect. These threads will provide wonderful effects in your machine embroidery. Stitches with long floats like a satin stitch exhibit a smooth visible surface of color. Textured fill stitches in a monochromatic colorway provide a beautiful blending effect. Short stitches used in quilting or outlining a design offer a more dotted effect with lots of variation in the color theme.

TIP: When stitching on solid fabrics, it is best to avoid a spool with an exact color match to prevent areas that look like a void of thread. Patterned fabrics pair extremely well if your goal is blending the thread with the fabric. Variegated thread offers an interesting accent to wearable art and home décor as well as fun accents to larger embroidery designs with the color transitions and pattern intervals.

METALLIC THREAD

Mettler Thread

Metallic thread has been used throughout history to create striking details on everything from clothing to home décor. While metallic threads once featured real metals that were hard to care for and did not last, our modern metallic threads offer the look of metal created with a synthetic thread wrapped in bits of foil. Metallics come in solid metal colors, such as gold, silver, and copper, along with bold jewel tones and even variegated spools for amazing results.

This thread is the one most embroidery enthusiasts struggle with. As someone who has sewn hundreds of spools, I share that it was not always that way. Many avoid it because tension problems frequently cause thread breakage, but with a few metallic usage tips, your stitching will be flawless. When using metallic thread:

- Slow the machine speed to reduce friction on the thread.
- Use a metallic needle that has an eye specifically designed for the metallic thread.
- Loosen needle tension if needed and use a spool net to keep the thread from shooting large loops off the spool.
- Use the round spool dial on top of a vertical spool. Make sure there are no burs on the spool cover, so the thread does not catch. Sand off if necessary.

Metallic threads really make embroidery pop. This array of thread spools shows a variety of colors.

- My top secret trick: In the machine settings, turn off the automated thread clipping function between thread jumps. The automatic cutter pulls on the thread when cutting and rethreading the needle between stitches. The tension on the thread often causes it to stretch and pop back out, resulting in an unthreaded needle or broken thread. This is a no-fail solution!
- Care for your metallic thread by avoiding high direct heat when pressing that can dull the sheen and luster.

OTHER THREAD

There is an array of decorative threads with specialty features, including textured threads and yarns, denim threads, and even glow-in-the-dark embroidery. Enjoy the features they bring to your projects.

PRE-WOUND BOBBINS

Bobbin thread for machine embroidery is different than what is used in other sewing projects. Bobbin thread is designed to be finer, which helps reduce bulk in embroidery. Its lighter weight, compared to the top thread, assists in creating the necessary tension to pull the upper threads to the back of your project. When bobbin thread is pulling to the front of your embroidery project, adjusting the machine tension or changing the bobbin may be necessary. You will wind the bobbins that come with your machine with bobbin thread, but the exception might be a sheer fabric, where you will need to use the same thread as the embroidery to obtain a match from the front to back of the project.

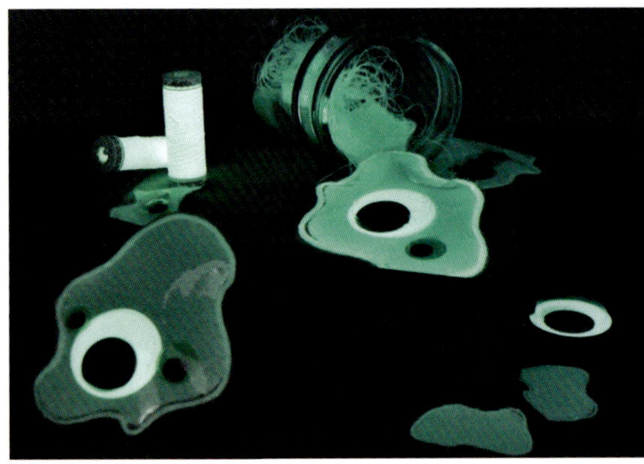

Glow-in-the-dark threads are fun for kids, outdoor designs, home décor, or a fun logo on a hoodie or T-shirt.

Pre-wound bobbins add a level of time-saving convenience, eliminating the step of winding your own bobbins that is especially handy for large projects or those in business. The tight weave often means it holds a larger quantity of thread with consistent tension. To use a pre-wound bobbin, check your machine manual for the type of pre-wound and size needed. Additionally, your machine may have a special setting for the bobbin case or bobbin sensor with the pre-wound.

The standard pre-wound bobbin will come in a plastic or paper-sided bobbin. Certain bobbin sensors may not detect the paper bobbin, requiring

Pre-wound bobbins feature a finer thread, which reduces bulk on the back of the embroidery design.

removal of the paper sides. Other machines work fine with the paper sides. While the paper acts like a spacer to prevent the bobbin from skipping around, you may have to experiment with your machine for best results. Whatever bobbin you are using, make sure it is wound correctly and does not have any loose or looping threads.

Thread Tips

- **Use a vertical spool pin with a spool cap.** This is so the thread moves away from the spool and does not catch as it comes off the spool.
- **Remove burs.** Make sure there are no burs on your spool caps or thread guides that the thread might catch on. Use a fingernail file to remove if necessary.
- **Have extra spools for larger projects.** You do not want to run out of a main color. Create a sample of the design to gauge how much of a spool will be used. For example, I created a rose-embroidered gown, and each motif required two spools of embroidery thread and a single pre-wound bobbin. The design totaled over 100 spools of embroidery thread alone.
- **Common colors.** Purchase larger spools of core colors that are used regularly, such as white, black, red, navy, gray, and blue to name a few.
- **Care instructions.** Pay attention to any unusual care, washing, or pressing instructions discussed for specific thread types. For example, avoid heavy pressing and steaming of threads with high sheen.
- **Bird's nest.** Wads of thread on the underside of a project are commonly called a "bird's nest" in sewing. While they do not happen often, if you embroider for any amount of time, you will encounter a bird's nest. When the upper thread tension is loose and not going in the tension dial correctly, this can cause issues with stitch formation. When threading the machine, make sure the presser foot is in the up position, opening up the tension disk that allows the upper embroidery thread to properly insert into the dial for best upper tension. Use a tightly wound bobbin and clean the bobbin case from any loose threads. Lastly, review design density, needle selection, and correct hooping, all of which prevent the dreaded bird's nest.
- **Clean your machine.** Remove any bits of thread that may be hiding.

Some projects (like the gown on page 76) require multiple spools to complete the project based on the size of the spool and the quantity of embroidery.

Make a small inventory of your own bobbins so they are ready when you have an embroidery session.

Needles

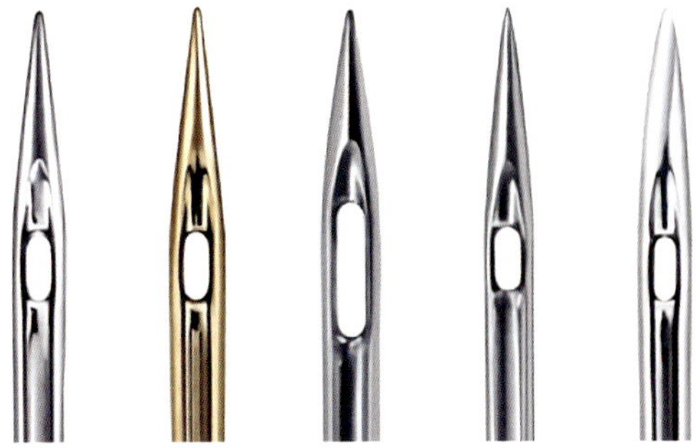

(Left to right) Ball point embroidery, titanium ball point, metallic, microtex/sharp point, and universal point.

SCHMETZ Needles and Euro-notions

Using the correct needle for any sewing project is imperative for successful results and is all about the right combination of needle size, thread, and application. An embroidery needle has a larger eye for the thread to pass through during rapid stitch formation. We now know to use the smallest hoop necessary for embroidery, but it is also best to use the smallest needle necessary to reduce the size of the hole puncture into the fabric during stitching. Remember, the needle is going in and out of the fabric at rapid speed hundreds and even thousands of times in the creation of an embroidered design.

Rhonda Pierce, from SCHMETZ Needles, the leader in machine needles, provided some interesting insight into the machine needles we use today. The most common size in embroidery is 75/11. SCHMETZ embroidery needles are available in chrome and titanium nitride (gold). Both are available in sizes 75/11 and 90/14. Other features of the SCHMETZ embroidery needle are a medium ball point and wide groove.

SCHMETZ chrome was introduced to the North American marketplace in 2017. With eight needle types in the most popular sizes, the benefits of chrome are its resistance to heat and wear. There is less resistance to the needle penetrating through fabric, and thread passes through the needle eye with less stress, making them ideal for embroidery. SCHMETZ chrome needles became immensely popular, so in 2020, all SCHMETZ needles transitioned from a nickel finish to chrome except titanium nitride (or nonstick) needles. For machine embroidery needles, Rhonda's best tip is that "needles do not last forever. Be prepared to change the needle. Using a fresh needle is the easiest way to elevate stitches."

While this is the same design on both leather and a tweed suit, different needles were needed for the unique base material.

THE ANATOMY OF A NEEDLE AND NEEDLE TYPES

The needle is an intricate tool in the formation of embroidery. The parts that affect needle selection include the tip, eye, shaft, and scarf. The **eye** is the small opening toward the end of the needle. As the Needle Eye Comparison diagram shows, the embroidery eye is enlarged compared to a regular sewing needle, allowing more space so there is less stress on the thread passing through the eye. Heavier threads benefit from this additional space because reduced friction on the fibers prevents breakage.

The thickness of the middle part of the needle, or **shaft**, determines the size of the needle. The area on the back side, right above the eye, is called the **scarf**. It is a groove where the machine bobbin hook passes the bobbin thread through the needle. In stitch formation, the bobbin hook catches the thread from the needle scarf, creating the loop that forms the stitch. Heavier threads need a bigger scarf for the thread to rest on, so pair a larger needle size with heavier threads and a smaller size for smaller threads.

The **point** or **tip** at the end of the needle is what goes through the fabric. You will select the tip that pairs best with your fabric selection. General descriptions of needle tips include ball point, sharp, topstitch, and universal.

- **Ball point:** The ball point has a rounded tip and prevents holes and raveling by going in between the fabric structure or knit looping, making them ideal for knits and stretch fabrics.
- **Sharp:** This is for precision and high-thread-count fabrics that have more threads per surface area like fine linen or dense cotton.
- **Topstitch:** The needle has an elongated eye, providing less stress on the thread as it passes through the eye. According to SCHMETZ,

NEEDLE ANATOMY - 130/705 H

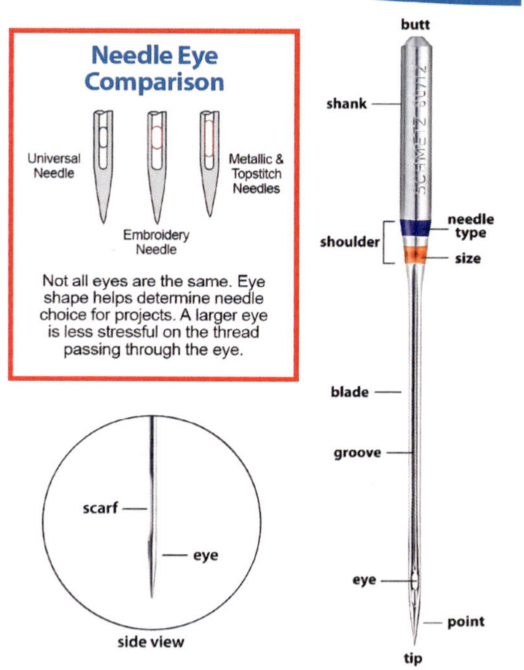

SCHMETZ Needles and Euro-notions

COLOR CODING

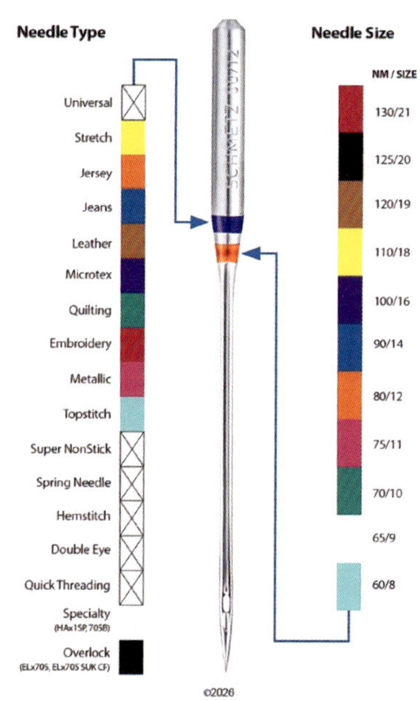

the topstitch needle is useful for sewing with metallic, heavy, multiple, and even poor-quality threads. It has a slightly rounded point.

- **Universal:** A popular needle choice for machine embroidery and the most common needle point is universal, which works on most fabrics.

SCHMETZ embroidery-specific needles include super nonstick, super universal, embroidery, and topstitch. While leather or metallic needles may be needed for special threads or materials, often the combination of stabilizers negates the need for a variety of specialty fabric needles since the goal is embroidery. Achieve perfectly straight and even stitches when using a straight stitch needle plate. As suggested, take some time to create stitch samples to see how your machine interacts with the fabric and needle combination.

All these elements work together for successful and seamless stitching. You can see why a new, sharp, unbent needle is imperative for all stitch formation components to work together for precision stitching. Change your needles often!

NOTE: Different embroidery machines may be designed to work best with a specific embroidery needle size. Reference your machine guide for those specifications.

NEEDLE TIPS AND TROUBLESHOOTING

- **Small needles:** Use the smallest needle possible to match your thread selection.
- **Matching needles to projects:** Choose needle type based on the fabric and threads used. Heavier designs need a larger needle going through layers of fabric, stabilizer, and thread. Dense designs may need a sharp needle to penetrate layers of stitching. Lighter weight fabrics require a smaller needle size and shaft to scale down the hole created when stitching the fabric.
- **Replacing:** Change your embroidery needle frequently to prevent skipped stitches and ensure the best stitching of the design. A fresh needle can usually fix issues like broken threads and bad tension. A dull needle does not allow the machine mechanisms to work efficiently. Plan to replace your needle at least one time per project.
- **Good habits:** While different fabrics and finishes may affect how quickly a needle becomes dull, a good rule of thumb is to change the needle at the beginning of each project. It is an inexpensive way to avoid common embroidery problems.
- **Cleaning:** If you use spray adhesive and your needle gums up, you can wipe it clean with rubbing alcohol.

Let's Talk Tension

One final setting in the embroidery formula is the tension of the thread in the machine. You will need to reference your manual for any specific dials or adjustments, but the following tips will help you in the final setting up of your design:

- **Tension:** If the bobbin thread is visible on the top of the design or the top thread is pulling into the bobbin, then adjust your machine tension.
- **Bobbin case screw:** Subtle changes can be made by adjusting the bobbin case screw micro amounts (reference your machine manual).
- **Check your tools:** Do not forget a new sharp embroidery needle. Reference the pre-wound bobbin notes if using those (see page 62).

With a well-thought-out design, you are ready to stitch. Each machine has different specific settings for embroidery, so we cannot cover them all here. Reference your manual if you have not already for attaching your embroidery hoop, adjusting the speed, and any machine-specific sewing tips. The biggest adjustments in embroidery are the needle, stabilizers, and slight tension modifications, which are all easy to adjust with a little practice.

CHAPTER 7

Project Guides

Companion patterns, embroidery designs, projects downloads, and video lessons featuring these projects are available at www.designerjoi.com.

The design possibilities are endless when it comes to machine embroidery, and the key to a successful project is customizing each element of your project. Like a recipe for baking, you will select your "ingredients" and evaluate the combination to see how it works for you. Make subtle adjustments as needed, and the more you use your new knowledge of embroidery skills and how to make the best selections, the more your experience and knowledge grow. There will be some scenarios that require special treatments, but most embroidery involves a simple selection of the design, correct stabilizer and thread choices, and proper hooping, then you can stitch away.

It may take a little extra time up front, but making a sample will ensure optimal results. You will then have a sample recipe for future projects that will be a time-saver moving forward.

The following project guides are an outline of some of the most popular embroidery applications. You will want to customize the projects to your embroidery machine and project scenario; make sure to follow any special instructions specific to the products or sewing patterns you are using. If you do not see your exact embroidery scenario, simply follow the checklist on page 68 and use the sample card on page 31 to make all your selections. Whatever your embroidery passion, your personalized designs will be treasured for years to come and will build your lifelong love of machine embroidery.

The embroidery design can be stitched as an outline or appliquéd with matching or contrasting fabric to decorate a table runner, combining both sewing and quilting skills.

CHECKLIST

Now that we have covered all the core elements for successful embroidery selections, here is a final checklist for setting up your project:

	Determine your project. Select the design and fabric or embroidery blank.
	Make sure the design size and density work with your fabric.
	Determine if the fabric needs any special surface treatment, such as an interfacing.
	Select the stabilizer that will best support the design and pairs with the fabric.
	Pick your desired thread colors and any specialty threads you might use.
	Choose the correct needle for the threads, fabric, and design.
	Hoop the project and use any special hooping techniques that might be needed.
	Evaluate your machine. Make sure it is set up correctly for embroidery: settings, new needle, thread, etc.
	Make a stitch out of the design on sample fabric to evaluate the settings. Adjust settings if necessary.

PROJECT 1

Basic Monogram Dress

TECHNIQUE: Adding embroidery during project assembly

A monogram is a design usually featuring initials embellished with additional decorative elements, such as a border or scrolled edges to the letters. This popular form of embroidery is wonderful for gifts and a variety of embroidery projects like towels, pillowcases, and children's clothing. It is also a suitable place to start your embroidery journey using a stabilizer that makes it easy to sew fabric like cotton, linen, voile, or bamboo.

SUPPLIES

- Lightweight cotton, linen, or voile
- Dress sewing pattern
- Embroidery pattern
- Rayon or polyester embroidery thread
- Embroidery stabilizer (suggested: light to medium tearaway, fusible mesh, or medium-weight tearaway)

PLACEMENT SUGGESTIONS FOR MONOGRAM PROJECTS

There are suggested placement guidelines for embroidery; however, you really can add a monogram anywhere you want. The size of a garment affects the placement of stitching as well as the overall scale and proportion of the design. Page 50 lists recommended spots for monograms and embroidery.

PLACEMENT ON A PREMADE ITEM

When adding a monogram on a premade child's garment or smaller item, you will have to determine what hoop will fit the project and build the design out from there. Select a monogram that fits the project and the hoop. When placing the hoop on the machine, your project may have a different orientation when viewing in the machine. You may need to use basic machine editing features, such as rotating the design, so that it stitches out facing the right direction.

PROJECT ASSEMBLY

For the child's embroidered dress or any project sewn from a pattern, you will need to determine when to add the embroidery to the pattern piece while assembling the garment. In general, it is best to apply any detail to a flat fabric block, prior to cutting out your pattern piece. This provides ultimate flexibility in placement and ease of hooping. Add the monogram to the flat bodice front before joining the back pieces or attaching the skirt.

1. Ensure the monogram fits the size and scale of the child's pattern piece and overall garment being made.

2. Cut a rectangle of the fabric slightly larger than the pattern piece and larger than the embroidery hoop. Mark the center. The shape of the pattern piece is cut out after adding embroidery to the fabric.

TIP: Make a chalk outline of the pattern piece on the fabric or baste around the pattern to determine precisely where the monogram will stitch on the fabric. This is helpful if placing the monogram around a specific detail of the fabric surface or pattern.

3. Add interfacing to the back surface of the fabric to address any issues with the fabric surface if necessary. This stable cotton fabric does not require any additional support. A fabric with stretch may require stabilizing the structure to prevent distortion when hooping or adding embroidery.

4. Cut and place the embroidery stabilizer on the back of the fabric and hoop together, centering the outline of the pattern. Mark where the center of the monogram is to be placed.

5. Set up your embroidery machine with selected thread, needle, and bobbin. In your embroidery, set up the screen and move the needle placement so the design begins at the center of the monogram location. The key to this design is all about the placement of the design.

6. Stitch out the monogram.

A simple monogram is the ideal beginner project for trying machine embroidery.

7. Remove from the machine and carefully remove the fabric from the hoop. Tear or cut away the stabilizer at the back side of the monogram and press.

8. Place the original pattern piece on the embroidered fabric. Retrace the outline of the pattern and cut out the pattern piece.

9. Finish the dress assembly according to your pattern sewing instructions.

TIP: If you are making an embroidery sample to evaluate all the machine settings, use the tests to make a matching pillow, small tote bag, or as the actual stitch out for your child's dress.

VARIATIONS ON A DESIGN

Add lace (page 74) to the hem of this dress or add a monogram to a premade piece following the easy guide on page 83. To monogram towels in the same fashion, follow the project on page 79.

PROJECT 2

Sewing Pattern Bodice Appliqué

TECHNIQUE: Stitch-and-trim appliqué

Appliqué adds texture and interest to a design by layering fabric pieces onto a larger area of the embroidery project. First, outline stitches secure the appliqué fabric to the main piece. Next, various decorative embroidery stitches—like satin or blanket stitches—are applied to finish off the design. Appliqué-specific designs save time by eliminating large areas of fill stitches, and most fabrics can be used, thus expanding design possibilities. The template method or the stitch-and-trim process is the most common. Freestanding motifs and laces are considered a variation on appliqué; however, these are covered on page 74.

SUPPLIES:

- Appliqué fabric
- Embroidery pattern
- Embroidery thread
- Embroidery stabilizer (suggested: fusible tearaway adhesive, spray adhesive for backing the appliqué, and medium tearaway for backing the hooped project)
- Fine-point or curved shears

FABRIC CHOICE

Some designs require a lot of textures that embroidery stitches cannot fully replicate. By using textured and printed fabrics, the appliqué helps achieve the desired effect and adds more depth to a project. For example, the colors and textures in nature work well with printed fabric appliqué rather than relying on the stitches solely to replicate something like a rock or tree bark.

PROJECT ASSEMBLY

The bodice pattern appliqué design, featuring the basic bodice sloper shape, pays homage to garment sewing through the ages and my love of flat pattern design. This appliqué uses the popular stitch-and-trim process, which is fun, quick, and easy.

1. Determine the size of the fabric to be embroidered according to the pattern instructions. Mark the area where the center of the embroidery design will be placed.

2. Before cutting the pattern piece, add an additional 2" (5.08cm) buffer to all sides prior to embroidery. For example, if a finished quilt square measures 10" x 10" (25.4 x 25.4cm), the buffer makes it 12" x 12" (30.5 x 30.5cm). If necessary, add additional space to all edges, making an easily hooped layer of fabric.

3. Cut the stabilizer(s) to the same size as the prepared pattern piece and hoop all layers together. The slightly smaller appliqué fabric will not be hooped.

4. Set up the embroidery machine for the design and carefully attach the hoop to it. Place the appliqué fabric on top of the hoop. If needed, use a scant amount of spray adhesive, but the fabric will usually stay in place on its own.

5. Stitch the design outline on the appliqué fabric. Stop the machine if it does not automatically stop.

6. Carefully remove the hoop from the machine, but **do not** unhoop the fabric.

7. With fine-point or curved shears, trim around the outside of the bodice embroidery outline, removing the excess.

8. Place the hoop back in the embroidery machine and finish stitching the design. The stitching covers the trimmed edge.

9. Square up and trim down the design after embroidery. Remove any stabilizer and pressing applications for a perfectly embroidered pattern piece.

TIP: If the appliqué fabric has stretch, add a fabric interfacing like a fusible knit or fusible weft to stabilize the stretch prior to adding the embroidery stabilizer. **My favorite tip:** On lighter and fine fabrics, add a single layer of nylon netting under the appliqué to add an additional support grid to designs with delicate details.

ALTERNATE TECHNIQUES

Variations of appliqués use a template where the shape is cut out prior to stitching. The machine will stitch the outline, the appliqué (with an adhesive backing or spray adhesive) is positioned and stitched down with no trimming needed. Alternately, reverse appliqué features the decorative fabric sandwiched between the surface fabric and stabilizer. After the outline is stitched, the surface fabric inside the outline stitching is trimmed away to reveal the contrasting fabric underneath and finished with a decorative stitching.

PROJECT 3

Embroidered Lace

TECHNIQUE: Freestanding embroidery without fabric

Embroidered lace is a wonderful use of embroidery, making designs solely comprised of thread and a layer of stabilizer. The lace design features a base foundation of stitches that supports the overall motif and design once the stabilizer is removed. For larger pieces, lace yardage is created by linking motifs in a continuous fashion using a larger hoop, multiple hoopings, or sewing smaller motifs together after they are stitched. Individual appliqués for jewelry, ornaments, gifts, or garment accents feature a single motif, making this a very versatile option for embroidery.

SUPPLIES:

- Embroidery pattern
- Embroidery thread
- Heavyweight water-soluble stabilizer
- Bucket or container (optional)
- Towel
- Spray starch

THREAD REQUIREMENTS

When making massive quantities of dense embroidered lace, stitch out a single motif to determine how much thread is needed (this includes the bobbin) and purchase enough for your project plus extra ahead of stitching so you do not run out. For example, one motif may require a full spool, and stores do not often have large quantities of individual colors if the project requires multiples. For large projects, consider buying large industrial spools like those for multi-needle machines.

PROJECT ASSEMBLY

Some designs may require a double layer of stabilizer for best results. Evaluate your combination to find the right combination for your machine and projects.

1. Set up the machine and wind bobbins with matching thread. Wind several bobbins prior to creating the motif. When making multiple motifs, use the largest hoop on your machine and duplicate the design in the embroidery setup screen.

2. Hoop the water-soluble stabilizer. If using a layer of netting or sheer fabric, place the stabilizer behind the fabric.

3. Stitch the embroidery pattern. If making a continuous lace border, duplicate the pattern as many times as possible in one hooping, linking them together. Remove the item from the hoop, trim away excess stabilizer, then rehoop, carefully marking where the pattern can resume stitching.

4. Remove the lace from the hoop after stitching or the final hooping.

5. Trim away the excess stabilizer from around the back side of the motifs.

6. Remove the water-soluble stabilizer. For a light application of stabilizer, simply rinse the motif under warm water. For a heavy application, fill a basin with warm to hot water and let the embroidery soak according to the manufacturer's suggestions. Pour out the water and rinse again with warm water. If the water seems gummy or the lace is sticky, then repeat soaking the design to remove all the residue. This may take a couple of rinses for large quantities.

7. Shape the design. Place a large towel flat on the table with the lace on top. Shape the lace and pat dry with a towel on top. Press flat with a warm iron and let air-dry if needed. Apply stiffener, such as a spray starch, for a crisp look.

ALTERNATE TECHNIQUES

If a design cannot support the stitches, you will need a sheer layer of fabric as a base layer. Netting comes in most colors for a hidden layer of support. Make appliqués using this method. These are cut out and applied to fabric, making a garment look like embroidery was added to the fabric when it was made separately.

PROJECT 4

Customizing Fabric

TECHNIQUE: Using embroidery on fabric or yardage for garments

Embroidered fabrics are popular in fashion and garment sewing thanks to endless thread colors and embroidery designs. A fully customized fabric is easier than ever to create for that one-of-a-kind design. Based on the complexity of the embroidery design and application, the entire fabric piece may be embroidered prior to cutting out the pattern pieces or individual pattern pieces may be cut out and embroidered, paying careful attention to motif placement once the design is sewn together. Embroidered fabric is a little more time consuming, but the results are well worth the effort.

SUPPLIES:

- Fabric plus extra for the project
- Garment sewing pattern
- Embroidery pattern
- Interfacings for the fashion fabric (optional)
- Embroidery thread
- Embroidery stabilizer (suggested: tearaway, medium fusible mesh, or heavyweight cutaway)

PROJECT ASSEMBLY

On any garment hooping, you will need a piece of fabric much larger than the actual pattern piece. Due to the large surface area, combination of stabilizers, quantity of stitches, and other variables unique to each project, there may be some shrinkage in the design. The bigger the fabric piece, the more it may be affected.

For Allover Fabric Design

Multiple yards of fabric are cumbersome to hoop and might pull on the embroidery frame, causing tension issues, so it is best to work in smaller increments. Ideally, you will work on one pattern piece at a time, but some pattern pieces, such as a skirt or gown, are inherently larger. Some designs require continuous hooping prior to sewing the fabric for correct placement; a bodice would be an example.

Evaluate your pattern layout and determine what pieces can be cut individually and which, if any, need continuous yardage. For the larger areas, allow additional space around the pattern piece. For some garment designs, it may be possible to add seams to a garment that are not in the original pattern. This is usually hidden with embroidery and will allow stitching of smaller, more manageable pieces.

For Individual Pattern Pieces

Cut out the paper pattern piece and place it on the fashion fabric, addressing any details of the fashion fabric that should be incorporated into the design. Cut a rectangle significantly larger than the final pattern piece to allow for hooping and any shrinkage that may occur.

Continue for Allover and Individual

1. Take time to plot out each piece before doing any stitching. Have a plan for lining up all the motifs, if needed, and pattern pieces. Note: Some seam lines will not have embroidery, and you may use a combination of stitching directly on the fabric and making appliqué to hand stitch over the seam lines; the viewer does not know the difference. Some areas of a garment are not able to have the embroidery

LAYERING DESIGNS

Layering embroidery designs is an effective method for creating fabric. Apply a smaller, more open background design (such as the gold leaves shown here) to fill more of the surface area of the fabric. This can be stitched all over the fabric and is easy to duplicate, as the motifs may not need to match. Add more detailed motifs (such as the roses) to the fabric, spaced further apart for extra dimension to the fabric. These intricate motifs may feature thread changes or the same color for a monochromatic effect.

A stitched-out sample of the design helps visualize how it will look on a specific garment pattern piece. The lines and arrows marked here help plot out design placement. Embroider as much of the designs on individual pattern pieces prior to garment assembly.

directly on top, such as dense seams, layers, or areas with things like metal boning for shaping. Garment embroidery is all about customizing different techniques to create that final project.

2. Mark the fabric pieces with any reference lines needed for lining up designs. If a design placement is random, it may not be as imperative, but for continuous patterns, stitch or baste a reference line for matching with the pattern. For any motifs, mark the center where a design is to be placed.

3. Cut large pieces of stabilizer to match the entire fabric piece or big enough to fit the hoop. Due to the larger surface area, it may be necessary to baste the layers together prior to hooping.

4. With pattern pieces, the fabric may be floated and not hooped so the design will be perfectly centered. In combination with the placement buttons in machine setup, determine the orientation of the embroidery and hoop so the pattern will match the embroidery machine. For example, if the top of a design is to the left side of the embroidery layout, then your hooped design needs to be placed so the top is hooped to the left. Or you will rotate the design to match the fabric. Be very aware of the placement of the design on the screen and how it should orientate on the fabric when stitching.

5. Once you have the pattern set and your fabric hooped, double-check that the motif will stitch where you want it. Then you can embroider.

6. Carefully remove the hoop from the fabric and remove any excess stabilizer. Lightly press the fabric and re-mark any placement reference lines for stitching. Rehoop the design.

7. Repeat the process until all the fabric is embroidered.

8. Remove any final stabilizer. Press from the back side. Place the pattern piece on top of the fabric and cut out.

9. Finish the garment assembly according to your pattern sewing instructions.

VARIATIONS ON A DESIGN

Add a flat background embroidery to the yardage, and create separate lace (page 74) or separate appliqués (page 72) for a three-dimensional look. When layering embroidery, the patterns become denser and more detailed. This layering adds depth, and in creative clothing design, you may want more than a single flat motif.

PROJECT 5

Towel Decoration

TECHNIQUE: Floating embroidery on fabrics with special surfaces

Towels and blankets are popular for embroidery projects because they are simple, fast, and make thoughtful personalized gifts. The fabrics for these projects as well as other specialty fabrics feature a lofty, fibrous nap or directional surface. The key to success for these projects is not to smash or damage the surface by applying a stabilizer topping and floating the item on top of the hooped stabilizer.

SUPPLIES:

- Towel, blanket, sweater, scarf, or specialty item
- Embroidery pattern
- Clear vinyl topping or wash-away stabilizer
- Heavy, stable cutaway stabilizer (suggested: mesh cutaway)
- Spray adhesive
- Embroidery threads
- Ball point needle for fabrics with stretch (optional)

Mettler Thread

TOPPING

Without a stabilizer topping applied to the surface of the fabric, the embroidery will sink into the surface texture, providing less than desirable results for the embroidery design. Refer to the stabilizer topping recommendations from page 41.

PROJECT ASSEMBLY

1. Mark where the center of the embroidery design should be located on the project. Mark any vertical or horizontal reference lines if necessary.

2. Hoop the backing stabilizer. Do not hoop your project, as it will damage the surface. The only item in the hoop is the cutaway stabilizer, which needs to be secure. It will not perforate like a tearaway, which would cause issues during embroidery. A self-adhesive tearaway stabilizer works well on towels.

3. Use a layer of spray adhesive on the hooped stabilizer. Reference the guideline points on the hoop and line up the placement lines from your project to them. Float the project over top of the hoop and press it to secure it to the stabilizer.

4. Set up the machine and insert the hoop, being careful not to bump or shift the floating project.

5. Place the topping on the surface of the project and stitch. Remove when finished.

6. Cut away excess stabilizer from the back side, but do not trim it too close. Leave a ½"–1" (1.27–2.54cm) buffer around the design to support it.

7. Carefully peel away the clear topping stabilizer from the border, leaving the design sitting on top of the fabric surface. If there are little bits of the topping stabilizer, you can remove them with the tip of an iron, but do not press the surface of the project.

Mettler Thread

VARIATIONS ON A DESIGN

Fabrics and projects that feature surface nap and lofty fibers include some of the following: monogrammed sweaters, fleece blankets, velvet, stretch velvet, specialty lace, and faux fur. These surfaces feature a nap with a distinctive direction to the way the fibers lie down. All pattern pieces are cut facing the same direction to avoid one side of a project with fibers going in one direction and the opposite in the other direction.

NOTE FOR SPECIALTY FABRICS

Knit fabrics will have stretch, and some specialty fabrics have a mechanical stretch to the weave of the fabric. The fabric needs to be secured before embroidering. Baste a layer of woven interfacing to the back of the fabric to secure the fibers. When you attach it to the hooped embroidery stabilizer, this will eliminate distortion in the hooping and floating process. Additionally, knits require a ball point needle when sewing to protect the stitch loop formation from unraveling.

PROJECT 6

T-Shirts and Sweatshirts

TECHNIQUE: Embroidering on T-shirt or sweatshirt material

Chances are you have numerous embroidered T-shirts or sweatshirts in your wardrobe. This type of embroidery is common and a wonderful way to make coordinating apparel for your local club, school, church, or community group. There are a few basic techniques to master that will ensure success every time.

SUPPLIES:

- T-shirt or sweatshirt
- Embroidery pattern
- Ball point needle
- Ruler
- Marking pen or tailor's chalk
- Embroidery thread
- Spray adhesive
- Cutaway stabilizer
- Neutral stabilizer (for T-shirts)
- Medium tearaway or cutaway stabilizer (for sweatshirts)
- Water-soluble topping

NOTE: Use a neutral stabilizer to blend into the front of the shirt with another on the back. There are also backing stabilizers that can be fused to the back of a T-shirt design, preventing the back side of the embroidery from irritating the skin.

PROJECT ASSEMBLY

1. Decide where to place the embroidery design; refer to the Common Embroidery Locations (page 50) or determine your own. Mark the center of the design location along with the vertical and horizontal reference points on your shirt with a marking tool. Placement is key to avoid a crooked or offset logo.

2. Add stabilizer to the back side of the shirt using spray adhesive or self-adhesive stabilizer. Since the garment is not flat, you will need extra help to hold the stabilizer while hooping. Lightly spray the cut piece of stabilizer, insert into the hoop, position behind the markings, and press in place.

3. Hoop the shirt. T-shirt material is lighter in weight than other fabric and can easily stretch or skew if hooped incorrectly.

3a. Unscrew the hoop screws enough so you do not need to force the hoop together, causing damage to the shirt.

3b. Line up the markings on the hoop with the placement lines marked on the project.

3c. Insert the inside hoop into the outer and tighten the screws. The T-shirt should be taut but not pulling.

3d. If your hoop comes with a plastic template, place on top to confirm that all the placement lines match.

4. Position the rest of the shirt away from the stitching area. Because the shirt is tubular and not flat, you will need to guide the outer edges of the shirt away from the center so it is not caught when stitching. Use tape, hand basting, or safety pins to anchor the excess toward the outer edges of the hoop away from the stitching surface.

QUALITY MATTERS

Not all T-shirts are created equal. While it might be tempting to choose a garment blank for a few dollars from a big box store, by saving a few bucks, you may encounter unforeseen frustrating issues in the embroidery process due to a poor-quality shirt base. Instead, look for a quality shirt that will support the embroidery design and withstand multiple wears and washings. Try a few brands and find one that is dependable on all your projects.

5. Float a layer of water-soluble topping on the surface of the hoop. A topping is ideal for T-shirt embroidery because it prevents stitches from sinking into the design.

6. Stitch the design. Upon completion, remove the T-shirt from the hoop. Carefully trim and remove the excess stabilizer.

KEEP IN MIND

If you find you are making large quantities of T-shirts, and chances are you might, then look into a hooping station for rapid, consistent hooping between stitch outs.

Mettler Thread

PROJECT 7

Embroidered Jacket

TECHNIQUE: Adding embroidery on ready-to-wear garments

Not every embroidery project will be a garment sewn from a pattern. Embroidery is a wonderful way to revive that forgotten apparel item in the back of your closet, update a garment staple, or repurpose a new treasure found at a thrift shop. Embroidery adds interest to the hem or entire side seam of jeans and leggings, adds stylish elements to a sleeve or jacket back, or subtle accents to collars and cuffs. Navigating what embroidery should be used and how it will be applied to these premade garments leads to some questions that will help make the right decisions for each individual garment.

SUPPLIES:

- Embroidery pattern
- Seam ripper
- Rulers
- Tailor's chalk
- Various stabilizers
- Embroidery threads

CONSIDERATIONS FOR PREMADE CLOTHING

I recommend opening the seams in the garment to access the area to be embroidered. Once it is stitched, sew it back up. The garment will look as if the embroidery was designed to be there. Sometimes there are limitations as to what area can be embroidered on ready-to-wear garments, but other solutions may present themselves too. The answers to these questions will help you select embroidery design and hooping options. Also, when selecting the embroidery design, make sure to use a mirror image when stitching the opposite side of the garment.

PROJECT ASSEMBLY

Because each ready-to-wear garment is different in how it is constructed, the following steps are a general guide to adding embroidery and should be modified as needed for individual garments.

1. Evaluate the garment and determine where you want to add the embroidery. It is important to mark the placement prior to opening any seams.

2. Select a design that fits the desired embroidery area and determine what hoop size will fit in the allocated space. When selecting a design, consider the density of the design and ease of hooping. Sometimes multiples of a smaller design fit better using a smaller hoop rather than one big one.

3. Select a stabilizer that pairs with the fabric. Add interfacings on fabrics that need the stretch or yarns secured prior to hooping or stitching.

4. Before hooping, evaluate any elements of the garment that can be removed for better access, such as a pocket that can be sewn back on after embroidery. Another consideration is avoiding thick bulky seams or details like zippers and flat-felled seams that may cause needle breakage. Position the embroidery away from obstacles.

5. Prep the garment by opening any seams that will allow better access and ease of hooping.

6. Add the stabilizer, hoop the garment, and proceed to add embroidery.

7. Trim or tear away the stabilizers, sew up any open seams or linings, and enjoy.

TIP: Round hoops are best for clothing, are much easier to use in tight spaces, and provide even tension around the entire embroidery surface.

VARIATIONS ON A DESIGN

For jeans and legging embroidery, open the inseam or the seam without the flat-felled seam. This can easily be stitched shut after adding embroidery. The same applies to sleeves; by opening the lining and side seam, more access to the side of a sleeve is provided. Instead of embroidering directly on the garment, especially for those smaller sized garments that are difficult to hoop, make an appliqué (page 72) and attach it by hand, which offers the same embroidered effect. Knit fabrics would be considered specialty fabrics. Tips for sewing specialty fabrics are included with Project 5.

Mettler Thread

The right color selection can make for a striking design.

PROJECT 8

Embroidering Leather

TECHNIQUE: Adding embroidery to unconventional materials

Adding embroidery to leather may seem challenging because it is not a woven or a knit. Additionally, skins come in organic shapes because they come off an animal, unless you're using a faux leather. However, leather is not any more difficult to sew than other materials with the correct selections in stabilizer, hooping, and design. Types of leather include cowhide, deer or pig suedes (these are softer and may have some stretch or give), lambskin, buckskin, faux, and unique things like alligator and snake. The simplified shape and design of most leather projects is enhanced with the machine embroidery thread and design.

This leather bodice is a lifelike copy of a sewing machine featuring real buttons and working lights. The pattern was designed around the body; each piece was embroidered separately and joined together.

SUPPLIES:

- Light- to medium-weight leather
- Embroidery pattern
- Marking tool
- Leather embroidery needle
- Medium to heavy cutaway stabilizer
- Spray adhesive
- Polyester embroidery thread

WORKING WITH LEATHER

If you are new to leather machine embroidery, evaluate a sample on a scrap of leather and make any adjustments to your machine as needed. Cotton thread is not suggested for sewing leather in the top or bobbin because the finishes on the leather break down the cotton fiber. Make sure to use a leather needle. When stitching leather, the needle will create a hole every time it punctures the surface of the skin. The narrow features of the leather needle will help with the stitch quality.

PROJECT ASSEMBLY

Because the needle creates a hole every time it penetrates the leather surface, dense and thick embroidery designs are to be avoided. Instead, look for designs that are more open. For designs like dense flowers or motifs, I suggest making an appliqué and affixing it to the project with leather glue as an accent to the base embroidery layer.

1. Place the pattern piece on the leather to determine where the embroidery will be located. Ideally, place on the back side of the leather with the pattern right side down, then trace with a pencil or chalk just outside the pattern edge. If there is a surface feature that requires placing the pattern from the top, trace just outside the pattern edge with a pencil or light chalk. Since leather will not shrink, you can cut out the pattern piece before adding the embroidery or wait until after.

2. Lightly mark where the center of the design is located. Small adhesive stickers work well on leather.

3. The leather is hooped by floating over the hooped stabilizer. Lighter leathers like pig skin can be hooped traditionally, but the surface of the skin can be easily scratched, flattened, or damaged from the hoop. It is best to hoop the stabilizer, spray it with temporary spray adhesive, and float the leather over top. Make sure to line up the center of the piece with the center of the hoop and all vertical and horizontal reference lines.

4. Place the hoop in the machine and stitch out the embroidery design using a slower speed. Because of the bulk of leather, it is wise to lightly hold and guide the fabric on the hoop while it is stitching so you can monitor if it shifts.

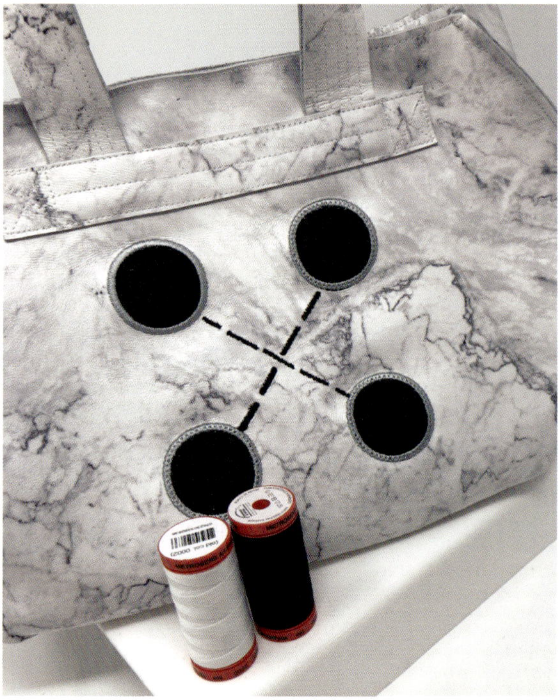

This fun leather bag is fully lined with an inside zipper and features button embroidery.

5. Upon completion of stitching, carefully remove from the hoop and trim away the excess stabilizer.

CARE INSTRUCTIONS

Leather does have some different care instructions. It cannot be washed, but a damp rag works for spot removal. Leather polish will keep your leather soft so it does not dry out, and any sewn leather project will last for years when well taken care of.

PROJECT 9

Embroidering Vinyl

TECHNIQUE: Adding embroidery to unconventional materials

Small clear vinyl purses, bags, and wristlets are popular for sporting events and concerts and are often required for admittance. So why not make your own? Clear vinyl is also used as an appliqué overlay, sewn into a bag, backed with a fabric, or stitched with a monogram or less dense design. Vinyl also comes in glittery finishes and heat-transfer variations. This is another fabric that has a few specialty considerations but is no more difficult to sew than other fabrics and adds a bit of whimsy to embroidery projects.

SUPPLIES:

- Vinyl
- Embroidery pattern
- Size 11 embroidery needle
- Medium wash-away stabilizer
- Fabric clips
- Polyester embroidery thread

WORKING WITH VINYL

Embroidery does create a hole in the vinyl when the needle penetrates the surface. It is like sewing leather, so the same guidelines work for vinyl. Use a small leather needle or a size 11 embroidery needle for smaller holes. There are different weights of vinyl, so evaluate a sample to determine what weight you like best.

PROJECT ASSEMBLY

Because the needle creates a hole every time it penetrates the vinyl surface, look for designs that are less dense. If you want dense flowers or other motifs, I suggest making them as an appliqué and affixing them to the project after embroidering the base design.

1. Use a single or double layer of water-soluble stabilizer on the back of the vinyl. Because vinyl is clear, you will want a stabilizer that is easily removable.

2. Hoop the stabilizer and the vinyl together. Floating the vinyl is also an option, but you cannot use spray adhesive, as it may leave residue on the vinyl. You need to cut a larger piece of vinyl, place it over top of the hooped stabilizer, clip it to the hoop, and support it with your hands until the design has stitched enough to hold in place.

3. Stitch the embroidery design with a matching thread in the bobbin case. Since the vinyl is clear, you will see the bobbin thread and will want it to blend with the top thread.

TIP: The embroidery machine should stitch the vinyl easily, but if you find your machine is not moving along the surface smoothly, place a layer of tissue paper or tearaway stabilizer on top of the clear vinyl that can easily be removed after sewing.

Oklahoma Embroidery Supply & Design (OESD)

This ornament contains a miniature scene covered with clear vinyl for an authentic snow globe look, sure to make your holiday décor merry and bright.

4. Remove the vinyl from the hoop after stitching and carefully trim away excess stabilizer.

5. Run warm water over the project to dissolve the stabilizer until there is no residue left.

6. Finish sewing the vinyl project but avoid using pins. They will leave a mark. Instead, use sewing clips if needed.

PROJECT 10

Embroidering Cork

TECHNIQUE: Adding embroidery to unconventional materials

Natural cork material is another unconventional material to use in embroidery, but it is also one of the easiest to stitch. Gaining popularity in sewing projects from bags, jewelry, aprons, and key chains to pillows, pouches, coasters, and ornaments. It is machine washable, inexpensive, and comes in a variety of colors.

SUPPLIES:

- Cork fabric
- Embroidery pattern
- Embroidery needles
- Threads
- Water-soluble stabilizer (for reversible designs) or tearaway stabilizer (for one-sided designs)
- Spray adhesive

WORKING WITH CORK FABRIC

No special needle is needed for cork, but a size 75/11 needle is a good option to keep the needle marks small. A variety of stabilizers pair well based on the project being made.

PROJECT ASSEMBLY

1. Select from a variety of densities in embroidery designs. Some thinner cork materials may need a less dense design, and thicker, more stable weights can manage denser motifs. Experiment with your cork material to find what stitches out the best.

2. Select a stabilizer for your project. Designs for coasters, key chains, and other reversible accessories use water-soluble stabilizers. Bags and pillows do not have a visible back side of the embroidery and are better suited for tearaway stabilizers.

3. Hoop only the stabilizer. Cork must be floated over the hoop and not placed in between the hoop layers, since it will damage the material. With the stabilizer hooped, use spray adhesive to affix the cork to the stabilizers.

4. Carefully place the hoop in the machine and stitch the design.

5. Carefully remove the hoop from the machine and remove the stabilizer from the design.

VARIATIONS ON A DESIGN

There are many unconventional materials that can be embroidered. Things like wrapping paper, shower curtains, ribbon, and canvas shoes can all be embellished with machine embroidery. With any material, the process is the same: evaluate the characteristics of the material; select an appropriate stabilizer, needle, and thread; and make a test sample. A sample stitch out rarely goes to waste, and you will gain valuable embroidery skills trying new things.

Oklahoma Embroidery Supply & Design (OESD)

PROJECT 11

Bonbon Purses

TECHNIQUE: In-the-hoop projects

In-the-hoop embroidery, as the name implies, is a design made completely in the hoop. These designs are smaller in scope, often no bigger than your hoop, making them an effective use of time; once removed, the embroidery design is complete or ready to join another part of a bigger project. For example, you can even add a zipper with your embroidery machine to make a purse. Things you can make in the hoop include, but are not limited to, cards, bookmarks, mug rugs, toys, jewelry, patches, bags, stuffed animals, and ornaments. There is a project for any style, from novel and whimsical to modern and classy.

Evy Hawkins

SUPPLIES:

- Purse sewing pattern
- Embroidery pattern
- Two fat quarters of cotton or other suggested fabric
- Self-adhesive wash-away stabilizer
- Thin foam stabilizer
- Sewing thread
- Embroidery thread
- Ribbon or premade purse handle

A NOTE ON THE BONBON PURSE

There really are infinite embroidery designs available for in-the-hoop creations, each with their own featured techniques. This lovely Bonbon Purse by my embroidery friend Evy Hawkins (A Bit of Stitch) is completely created in the hoop, featuring cutwork techniques, which remove fabric to make it lace-like, and a clean satin edge finish. Evy shared some of her favorite tips for this classy in-the-hoop design, which features a variety of embroidery applications, is petite in size for your favorite little one, and can be made at a larger size for adults.

These project instructions can work for any in-the-hoop purse, but if you want to match the examples shown here, the Bonbon Purse sewing pattern can be purchased at www.abitofstitch.com.

PROJECT ASSEMBLY

1. Select the project fabric. These purses can be made with quilt-weight cotton, silk dupioni, cotton, linen, or any light- to medium-weight fabric that can be washed. Evy loves using quilt-weight cotton and often quilts the pouch portion of her designs with her Baby Lock Sashiko quilting machine for a special touch.

2. Add the stabilizer. By using self-adhesive stabilizer, you do not need to get your hoop sticky with spray adhesive. Simply hoop the self-adhesive stabilizer release paper side up. Score the paper just inside the hoop with the tip of your snips or use a pin around the inside edge of the inner hoop. Pull up the release paper, and the sticky side is ready for you to adhere the fabric pieces to.

3. Hoop your project. Carefully mark the center of your fabric, place it in the hoop, and center using the hoop references as a guide. The fabric will float over the adhesive stabilizer.

4. Embroider using matching thread in the bobbin since the flap bottom may be visible once completed. The purse flap is completely created and finished in the hoop and then added to the purse. The purses and flaps are made sturdy yet soft and pliable by adding a layer of thin foam stabilizer right in the hoop during the embroidery.

5. After adding the embroidery, remove the purse flap from the hoop and trim away any excess stabilizer. The pouch portion of this purse is sewn together with a regular sewing machine.

Evy Hawkins

HOOPS FOR THE BONBON PURSE

This design features two varied sizes. The 5" (12.7cm) flap design fits most 5" x 7" (12.7 x 17.78cm) hoops and the 6" (15.24cm) flap fits most 6" x 10" (15.24 x 25.4cm) hoops.

PROJECT 12

Card Embroidery

TECHNIQUE: Adding embroidery to unconventional materials

Who does not love receiving a tangible card with a meaningful note? Inspired by my embroidery friend Pat, one of my favorite meaningful embroidery projects is card embroidery—suitable for anyone and any occasion. This simple yet versatile project utilizes a combination of the built-in embroidery machine features, including borders, outlines, and fonts.

SUPPLIES:

- Watercolor cardstock
- Embroidery pattern
- Heavyweight tearaway stabilizer
- Felt (optional)
- Embroidery thread

OPTIONAL DETAILS:

- Clear vinyl
- Specialty fabrics
- Additional embroidery patterns

PAT'S CARD INSPIRATION

My friend Pat Jones has a lovely ministry where she creates embroidered cards for all occasions. Having been on the receiving end of some of these, I can tell you it was so appreciated, and the timing was always impeccable. I knew each card was made especially for me, and sometimes a thoughtful gesture is more impactful than a big or expensive gift.

Pat says: "Make someone's day. Be creative so that when someone receives your handmade card, they will feel special knowing that you took the time to show you care."

PROJECT ASSEMBLY

1. For embroidering on paper, choose a design that is not very dense or stitch intensive. If you use a dense design, add a layer of felt on top of the watercolor cardstock to absorb the stitches.

2. Attach the stabilizer to the hoop and float the paper over top. Cardstock cannot be hooped. Do not use spray adhesive or sticky stabilizer since it will damage the paper.

3. If your machine can stitch a predesign outline or placement stitch, attach the felt and watercolor paper with the outline. This also adds a nice border to the card. Even if you plan to add a border to the card, this placement stitch will help secure the watercolor cardstock prior to adding the embroidery motif.

4. Utilize the built-in text or fonts stored in your machine to write any words, names, or messages. This project is great for using the basic machine editing and design features. Software programs also have many text options if you have one that you prefer, or you can even purchase alphabets online.

5. Add decorative features to the card after stitching, such as bows, sparkles, and more.

TIP: Cards are the ideal way to sample embroidery designs or use those embroidery sample stitch outs so nothing goes to waste.

VARIATIONS ON A DESIGN

Card giving is a bit of a dying art in the digital age, so revive it with a fantastic universal project that any embroidery machine can create. There is no size limit or investment in additional tools, supplies, or high-end machines. Card styles include common themes like thank-you, inspirational verses, birthday, and baby announcements, but other creative ideas include custom holiday cards, cards with embroidered photos, monograms, and even adding a layer of clear vinyl with little treasures like sequins or confetti in between.

Imagine the surprise of receiving a card in the mail that is not only handmade but also beautifully embroidered?

PROJECT 13

Embroidering Project Blanks

TECHNIQUE: Working with specialty blanks and tools

Embroidery blanks are like adding embroidery to a ready-to-wear sewn product. The advantage is that you can enjoy embroidering without having to create an entire sewn project. This saves time, and for those who do not enjoy sewing garments or other pieces, they can simply focus on creating embroidered elements for gifts, craft fairs, and an embroidery business. Blanks are designed with the ease of adding embroidery in mind, so they may have zippers or removable features for easy hooping and embroidery. Most companies that sell blanks offer tutorials and tips with projects designed specifically for their blanks.

SUPPLIES:

- Blank of your choice
- Embroidery pattern
- Embroidery thread
- Marking tool
- Spray adhesive
- Clamps, safety pins, or hoop tape
- Specialty hoops (examples: bag hoops, hat hoops, small item hoops, round hoops)

A pillow blank gives you the chance to add personalization and personality to your home décor.

This towel blank is now perfect for a kitchen.

SPECIALTY TOOLS

Types of embroidery blanks include shirts, towels, stuffed animals, jewelry, accessories, luggage tags, tote bags, market totes, travel accessories, hats, aprons, holiday items, bridal items, baby items, and more. There are many optional embroidery tools and accessories designed for working with many of these specialty blanks, now available to the home embroidery enthusiast. Check with your machine brand for additional accessories and compatible hoops.

PROJECT ASSEMBLY

Reference each brand or item for specific instructions, since the options are almost limitless. What follows are some basic guidelines and tips for sewing blanks of all kinds.

1. Make sure your embroidery blank fits the hoops for your machine and that you have all the correct parts. Many blanks use the basic hoops that come with your machine, but others may have some specific requirements. For example, hats need a specific driver and hoop for many machines, and some machines have a size limit.

TIP: If you plan to make multiples of a particular item, it is a good idea to purchase a few extras to evaluate all your embroidery settings until you have mastered that item. Some difficult-to-hoop items do take a little practice to refine your embroidery technique. Then use your reference sample card in the future for easy setup.

2. Evaluate the blank for specialty stitches, needles, threads, stabilizers, or design density. Make selections for each that will pair well with your blank for the best results. Use the sample card on page 31 to reference your selections.

3. Make sure the density of the embroidery design pairs well with the fabric of the blank. Check that the design fits the project and the hoop.

4. Set up your machine according to the selections in step 2.

5. Prior to hooping and stitching, remove any pillow forms, unzip, or adjust areas on the blank for ease of embroidery.

6. Some blanks will hoop with stabilizers, such as a pillowcase or shirt, and others will float over the hooped stabilizer, such as a blanket or stuffed animal. They will all vary.

7. Stitch your design.

8. After adding the embroidery, carefully remove from the hoop and remove excess stabilizer. Press items that will not be damaged by heat for a nice finish.

You can even embroider on a canvas bag blank!

PROJECT 14

Quilting

TECHNIQUE: Quilting with an embroidery machine

For quilters, adding quilting stitches to individual blocks or completed projects is necessary to hold all the layers together. Sending a piece out for quilting is expensive and labor intensive. An embroidery machine offers consistent stitches, saves time and money, and is versatile for individual blocks, appliqué, or the entire quilt top. Unlike random free motion techniques, quilting with an embroidery machine is very rhythmic and uniform.

SUPPLIES:

- Pieced quilt blocks or premade quilt top
- Quilt backing fabric
- Thin cotton quilt batting
- Lightweight tearaway stabilizer (optional)
- Embroidery thread
- Quilt-specific embroidery pattern
- Printable template
- Larger embroidery hoops or specialty hoops (suggested: magnetic)

Evy Hawkins

SELECTING EMBROIDERY PATTERNS

Theoretically, any stitch can quilt together layers of fabric, and you can apply techniques like appliqué as a method for quilting. For this project outline, we are going to reference embroidery patterns that are designed to stitch a quilt block. These are specialty designs that are purchased to be compatible with specific quilt block sizes.

PROJECT ASSEMBLY

When to quilt? In machine embroidery, you can hoop and quilt a single block, leaving the seam allowance for joining the pieces; or you can piece the entire project, layer, and then quilt. Exceptionally large quilts may be cumbersome to stitch at once, so working in smaller sections is advisable.

1. Layer the quilt pieces. The top is the pieced squares, the middle is batting, and the bottom is the backing fabric. A hoop will hold the area being embroidered together and is sufficient for a single block. Since you cannot use safety pins on the top when adding machine embroidery, it may be necessary to add basting stitches vertically and horizontally with a sewing machine or by hand.

2. Select a quilt embroidery pattern that fits the size of your quilt square or can be duplicated to fit. For example, a 10" x 10" (25.4 x 25.4cm) quilt block would use a single 10" x 10" (25.4 x 25.4cm) embroidery design. If the embroidery design is smaller and rectangular, it may require two embroidery patterns to quilt the square or four patterns of a smaller size.

3. It may be necessary to do a sample layout on test fabric prior to the final application to carefully plot out embroidery placement. If your design comes with a printable template, print off duplicates and place them on the full quilt top to plan the best layout for your project. Mark the center of each design with chalk as a reference for hooping. If you do not have a template, use a ruler to measure and plot out design placement.

4. Set up your machine with the top thread and use a thread in the bobbin that matches the back of the quilt. If possible, select a patterned or busy fabric back in combination with variegated threads. The color changes blend into the fabric, hiding embroidery thread stops and tie offs.

5. Hoop your quilt square. For an individual quilt block, a single hooping or a few hoopings (if you have a smaller hoop) will do the trick. It may not be necessary to baste as mentioned in step 1. For larger projects, expect multiple hoopings, so take care in placement and precision. Having marked references for the center of each design will be useful.

STABILIZER

Because true quilting patterns are basic stitches without much density, and because the quilt has several layers, it may be possible to eliminate a stabilizer. However, hooping a light- to medium-weight tearaway stabilizer offers stability for stitch formation. Evaluate the fabrics you are using and do a test sample to determine the best option for your project. If you can eliminate stabilizer, that saves the cost of that resource.

6. Stitch your embroidery quilting pattern. Remove the hoop, tear any stabilizer, press, and rehoop for any additional stitch outs. Make sure to press after each stitching, since the hoop will create a light fold or raised area from the frame.

7. After all the motifs are stitched, complete your quilt as your pattern describes, which is usually to add the binding.

TIP: Success in quilting with machine embroidery is all about planning and correct placement of the stitches.

PROJECT 15

Custom Patches

TECHNIQUE: Making embroidered custom patches

Patches are a decorative way to repair clothing, present awards and promotions, identify membership in an organization or team, celebrate holidays and events, and add customization to items that cannot be easily hooped and embroidered. Depending on their intended environment, patches may be serious or humorous, so have fun with them. Ordering premade custom patches often requires bulk quantities with large minimums, additional set-up fees, and high costs based on stitch count. You only need a few materials, so why not make them yourself? This is a perfect beginner in-the-hoop project using a single-needle home embroidery machine with so many possibilities.

SUPPLIES:

- 5" x 7" (12.7 x 17.78cm) hoop
- Embroidery pattern
- Patch twill fabric
- Tearaway stabilizer
- Patch stabilizer
- Spray adhesive or tape
- Hoop tape
- Fabric shears
- Curved shears
- Embroidery thread
- Chopstick or something similar

PROJECT ASSEMBLY

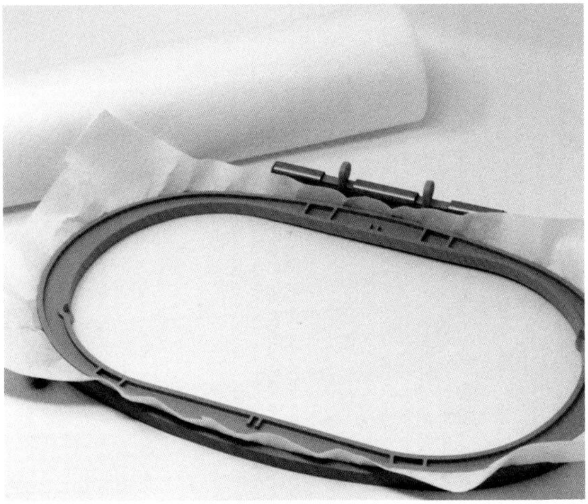

1. Cut a piece of stabilizer and hoop it. Float the patch twill fabric on the surface of the stabilizer with tape or spray adhesive.

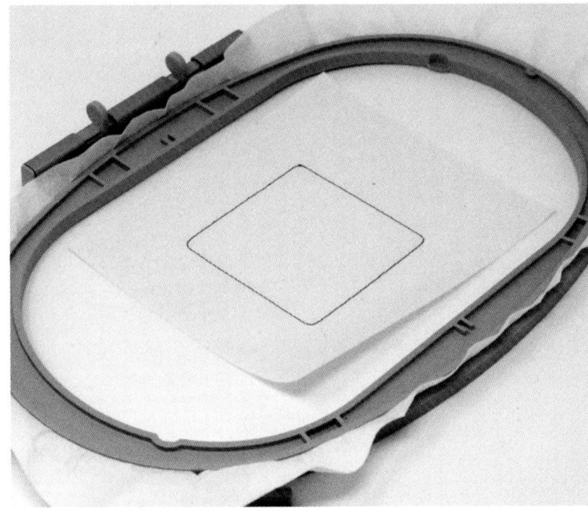

2. Stitch the outline for the patch template onto the twill.

3. Remove the hoop from the machine. Cut out the twill precisely on the stitching line, making the patch base.

NOTE: This tutorial was provided by Embroidery Legacy. They offer a large selection of patch sizes, borders, premade patch designs, and embroidery designs small enough for patch making that will have you well on your way to customized patches. Switch the color of fabric and thread for a completely customized look! Embroidery Legacy also offers a Patch Master Pro bundle that is an invaluable resource for patch making.

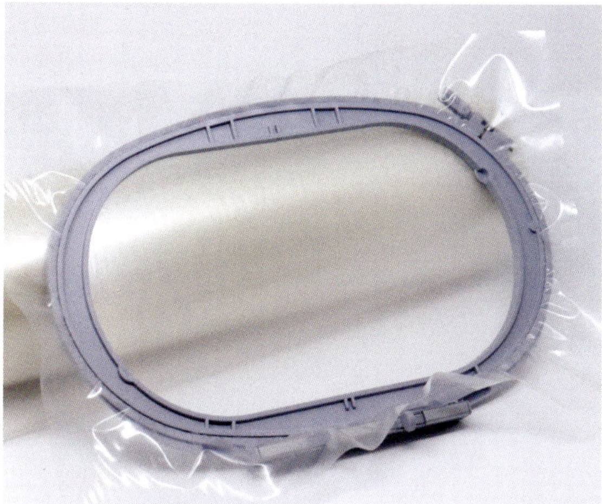

4. Hoop a piece of patch stabilizer. Place with the textured side facing down. Use hoop tape to hold the outer and inner hoop together, preventing movement during stitching.

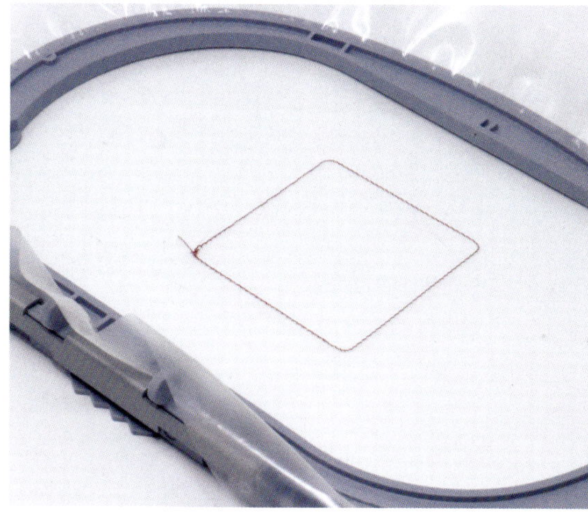

5. Place the hoop onto your embroidery machine. Stitch out the patch placement line onto the stabilizer.

6. Apply spray adhesive to the back of the patch base. The twill side is the front. Place it on the placement guideline. Stitch out the placement stitch around the patch base to hold it in place. Use a chopstick to guide the patch as it is tacked down.

7. Stitch the rest of your design. Remove the hoop and trim away any long threads from the back. Carefully press down on the border of the patch to remove it from the hooped stabilizer.

Troubleshooting

For perfect embroidery, follow all the best practices described in this book every time. After picking your project, you will select the corresponding embroidery design, needle size, thread, and stabilizer. These choices will help you avoid issues.

Making some sample stitch outs and sample projects will help you learn what your machine can do and gain a feel for how it works with the different combinations of materials. Your first line of defense for successful embroidery is sampling and using the sample card on page 31, which is a useful tool to record all your experiences. Sampling is never a worthless step or waste of time. This valuable tool will help you gain experience, and those sample projects can often be used for complementary smaller projects.

Even with all the testing and best practices, at some point you will encounter the most common embroidery issues. Here are some ways to navigate the problem:

NEEDLE ISSUES

- **Needle breakage:** Check needle placement. Use the correct size for your project.
- **Snags in the fabric:** Use a new, sharp needle.
- **Gummed-up needle:** Wipe with rubbing alcohol to remove spray adhesive.
- Refer to page 66 for more needle tips.

TENSION AND THREAD ISSUES

- **Visible bobbin thread:** Loosen the upper tension. Change the bobbin.
- **Skipped stitches:** Check the needle size, sharpness, and placement.
- **Thread breakage:** Make sure the upper thread is not caught on a spool pin or thread guide. Use the correct needle for the thread. Slow the embroidery speed. Change the needle.
- Refer to page 63 for more thread tips.

HOOPING ISSUES

- **Puckering:** Change stabilizer, evaluate the fabric characteristics, and rehoop.
- **Registration (the embroidery does not line up correctly):** Check the density of the design, needle, stabilizer, and hooping. Avoid reducing designs by more than 10 percent, as the size will cause issues with density.
- **Puckering design:** First check the fabric for any fabric interfacing or fabric stabilizer needs. Next check the design. It may be a result of poor digitization and too many thread stops on the back side of the design. If stabilizer adjustments don't work, you may need to select a different design or fabric combination.

TIP: Don't overlook good machine maintenance. This is also a front line defense for successful results. Clean your machine often, wipe the bobbin case, use a lint brush inside, and oil your machine. Change the needle at least once a project, or multiple times for larger projects.

These are just a few issues you can troubleshoot if they happen. Reference your machine manual for other machine-specific issues. Many newer machines have codes that pop up and tell you what the issue is. Overall, by following the information throughout this book, you will have a carefree embroidery experience.

Index

Note: Page numbers in **bold** indicate gallery photos, and page numbers in *italics* indicate projects.

About the Author

Laura Strain (Chase the Moment Photography)

Joi Mahon is the owner of the Sewing Factory in Sioux City, Iowa, and has been designing, fitting, and teaching sewing for over 25 years. She began sewing at a young age, transitioned into 4-H in the sixth grade, and was working as an assistant to a tailor at the age of 15. Joi has a degree in apparel design, merchandising, and production from Iowa State University, and she treasures all of her training and experiences both from the tailor shop and her mentors in the classroom.

She describes herself as a fashion entrepreneur with a wide array of sewing interests and endeavors. She has been featured in numerous sewing and craft magazines and online programs and has hosted Nancy's Notions Wardrobe Builder, *Threads* Magazine Complete Course on Interfacing, and Perfect Pattern and Fit Club.

Joi is a McCall's licensed pattern designer, Craftsy instructor (Fast Track Fitting and Fast Track Fitting in the Details), brand ambassador for Mettler Thread since 2011, and brand ambassador for OESD. She is part of the BERNINA Sewing Industry Alliance and travels to various stores and events to teach sewing, along with holding regular retreats in her onsite classroom at the Sewing Factory location.

Her first book, *Create the Perfect Fit*, was published by F+W Media and was followed by *Designer Joi's Fashion Sewing Workshop. The Ultimate Illustrated Guide to Sewing Clothes* and *Sewing Clothes: Elevate Your Sewing Skills*, published by Landauer, have been very well received.

Joi says, "The joy of sewing and design is that you have unlimited choices in what you make and how you make it. You also have the control to change the look, fit, and fabric when customizing your wardrobe. These options are not available in ready-to-wear, so this freedom is refreshing and exciting."

Joi has a line of patterns, fabrics, and resources available on her website and teaches free lessons every week on the Sewing Time Live program on the Designer Joi Mahon Facebook page.

Website: www.designerjoi.com
Facebook: DesignerJoiMahon
X: @DesignerJoi
Instagram: @DesignerJoi

Acknowledgments

A special thanks to Bobier Photography for the dragon quilt images; Pat Jones for the card stitch out; John Deer and Embroidery Legacy for the digitizing expertise, designs, and Custom Patches project; OESD for stabilizer tips, designs, and selection guide; Mettler Thread for threads, images, and expertise; Evy Hawkins for A Bit of Stitch images and the Bonbon Purses project; Kai Scissors for scissor images; SCHMETZ needles for needle expertise and images; and BERNINA Sewing Machines.